"IT WASN'T ABOUT YOU, JOAN."

A Cowgirl's Journey from Insecurity to Security, from Selfishness to Selflessness, from Fear to Faith

JOAN E. WURST

Copyright © 2023 Joan E. Wurst

All rights reserved. No part of this publication may be reproduced, distributed, or transmitted in any form or by any means, including photocopying, recording, or other electronic or mechanical methods, without the prior written permission of the publisher, except in the case of brief quotations in critical reviews and certain other noncommercial uses permitted by copyright law.

Scripture quotations marked (NKJV) are taken from the NEW KING JAMES VERSION®. Copyright© 1982 by Thomas Nelson, Inc. Used by permission. All rights reserved.

Scripture quotations marked (NIV) are taken from THE HOLY BIBLE, NEW INTERNATIONAL VERSION®. Copyright© 1973, 1978, 1984, 2011 by Biblica, Inc.™. Used by permission of Zondervan. All rights reserved.

Scripture quotations marked (TLB) are taken from The Living Bible copyright © 1971. Used by permission of Tyndale House Publishers, Carol Stream, Illinois 60188. All rights reserved.

ISBN: 978-1-7362821-6-8

Jacket Design: Shull Design

All photos courtesy of Joan E. Wurst.

Published by:
Missional Press
Nashville, TN
missionalpressbooks.com

Printed in the United States of America

INTRODUCTION

When I was 34 years old, I told my family and some friends: "If I should die at this age, don't feel sorry for me because I died so young. I have already lived more in these first 34 years than most people do in a much longer lifetime." I meant it. I had done many things and always gave those things my all. I felt I had probably done what I would do with my life.

Little did I know, of course, the things that lay ahead! That first 34 years held a lot of exciting times for me but the ride was just beginning in many ways. As of this writing God has more than doubled those years and the last 40 have been packed even fuller than the first 34. The main difference between those two periods could be who I lived each of those segments for.

There will be things in telling this story that will be painful for me to remember and to admit. It may seem I am being harsh with others. While much of this is difficult to admit, my husband and I are both willing to take the risks associated with letting others know just how awful we could be at times.

It is not my intention in these pages to make anyone look flawed in any way but rather to show the power of God to change a life. It is my desire that is what you glean from my experiences. The context I write is necessary because it is part of the total picture. My life is a depiction of how God can take an insecure, emotionally distraught, self-centered individual and change that individual into one who has confidence and boldness to do things she never imagined with her life.

I so wish I had been wise enough to do so many things differently, especially in the area of child rearing. As I looked at pictures to include in this work, I realized we had a lot of good times with our children, we gave them many things, and we took them many places, but how I wish I could have loved them as I now know how.

My desire in writing is to hopefully save others the years that I struggled alone with my hurts, fears, shames, and desires. The years that I learned slowly and painfully to find my love and security in Jesus; to trust and allow Him to make the needed changes in my life. It was a long, slow, lonely process.

My story could probably be separated into two categories such as "the early years seeking my own desires" and the later years "finding my true desires".

Through my journey I've had many different Bible verses that have helped me stay on the right path but one in particular sums up why I stayed on that path in spite of all the odds.

1 Corinthians 15:10: "But by the grace of God I am what I am, and His grace toward me was not in vain." (NKJV) I'm acutely aware of where I could have been or might be today without that grace. I'm extremely careful about judging others and I'm quick to say, "There, but by the grace of God, go I." It is so true.

ACKNOWLEDGEMENTS

There are many people to thank for my present position in life. My mother saw to it I was in Sunday school and church every week of my life until I was 15 years old. I remember the first Sunday school teacher that left a mark on me – the late Edna Gillis. What a dear sweet lady she was. I'm sure much of her teaching is responsible for the good things that have remained in my memory all these years. Lillian Fuessler, also gone to be with the Lord, was a godly woman who gave me direction and tangible help as a young wife and mother when I was desperate. She was the only person I could turn to during those dark days when I first got into impossible business and related situations.

That God chose to bring such spiritual giants into our lives as Rev. Clyde Davis, Sr. (who went to be with the Lord as this book was being written), Rev. Wes Aarum, an evangelist and spiritual giant in not just my eyes, Dr. Dale Linebaugh (who's biography gave me the inspiration to write my own) and Dr. Lew Sterrett, and their wives, to name a few is a blessing beyond description. They became some of our closest friends. What incredible spiritual help they have provided for me!

Wes' wife, Marge, became one of my dearest and most trusted friends and remains so to this day. Lew (director of Miracle Mountain Ranch a Christian youth ranch with horse related activities) and I share a common bond in training. His analogies of the relationship in our training of horses and our relationship to our heavenly Father have been of tremendous help to me in both my training of horses and personal spiritual growth.

My husband, Bill, was very supportive. He did not criticize a single thing I have written in this book, even if unflattering to him. He gave me the freedom, time, and space needed to write without complaint (almost). My sisters, Jean and Bev, provided emotional support and information that was helpful in my quest for answers to certain questions I had. Nancy Cook gave me the final push to seriously begin the work. Sandy Whipple first read my rough draft and encouraged me to continue and complete the manuscript. Linda Skelton, Bev, and Cindy Cairns, among others, took the time to read my work and encourage me to continue.

Marge Aarum heartily gave her approval of the work which meant a great deal to me. Since the time those friends first encouraged me, I have added years of living to it. That brought new friends to read and critique it for me as well. I received encouragement, correction, and advice from, amongst others, Bev (re-reading it); Jordan my dear friend and fellow horse and dog person, my friends, Sherri and Susie, and Dr. Dale Linebaugh. Dr. Lew Sterrett graciously wrote the Forward to the writing. Words cannot adequately express my gratitude for their help and support.

Thank you all and may God bless you.

ABOUT THE AUTHOR

Joan is a professional horse trainer, rodeo and futurity (a competition for horses of a certain age that have not previously competed) winning barrel racer, and rodeo winning team roper. She has been involved in rodeo and the training of horses and dogs for about 60 years. She is a Country gospel singer, songwriter, recording artist, author, and speaker, and has traveled for several years singing and speaking. She lived on a ranch with her husband of almost 56 years until his death in 2016. The mother of three, Joan is the grandmother of seven and the great grandmother of three.

In addition to breeding, raising, and training American Quarter Horses since 1965, she and her husband, Bill, ran a herd of Longhorn-cross cattle on their ranch, which they used for roping and team penning. Joan began raising American Lowline Angus cattle as well. Joan's interests include teaching and coaching barrel racing, horse training, trail riding, reading, writing, embroidery sewing, camping, and raising and showing Saint Bernards and Beagles.

Joan's children followed in her footsteps in rodeo, each having success in their respective events. Both of their sons, Randy and Scott, were talented ropers and horse trainers. Their daughter Laura Lee has made a successful career out of rodeo and training of horses with countless accomplishments and achievements in barrel racing in many associations. Laura Lee and her daughter, Mandi, also are accomplished professional trick riders, and performed in rodeos for a period of time as a specialty act.

In addition to the rodeo and other activities, Joan was the president and CEO of a site development company for 45 years.

FORWARD

This book is about loneliness and heartache. It is about peace and joy. It is about the process of healing and hope. It is a story of how God's love prevails through time, events, and circumstances and brings forth life from the hardened soil of the human heart.

It is the story of reconciliation. It is a living practical illustration of how a wise master builder sees the beauty in the unformed substance. It is how God takes a stone rejected by men and polishes it and refines it until it is precious in His sight and honorable before all. In the refining process we can see the waters of His faithfulness, love, and compassion washing away the hurts, the emptiness, and the confusion, bound up in the heart of a little girl. The washing and polishing continues throughout life, until there is purpose, understanding, and radiance.

It is the story of a lonely and grasping heart seeking the comfort and security that only God can provide. The events were difficult and sometimes overwhelming but were clearly no surprise to Him. Furthermore, it is a story of God giving a message and a ministry out of tragedy and despair. The comfort that was experienced in pain became the comfort given to others in trial. Hardships and depravity became the backdrop for proclaiming the excellencies of Him. This story is informative, transparent, courageous, and triumphant.

Dr. Lew Sterrett

Contents

Introduction iii
Acknowledgements v
About The Author vii
Forward viii
Chapter One: In The Beginning 1
Chapter Two: Moving 9
Chapter Three: Riding Time And Pony Therapy 15
Chapter Four: The Dance 20
Chapter Five: Childhood Ends – Abruptly 24
Chapter Six: Child Rearing 27
Chapter Seven: Home Sweet Home Number Two 32
Chapter Eight: The Race 36
Chapter Nine: Life – And Nearly Death 40
Chapter Ten: Priorities 45
Chapter Eleven: Another Brush With Death 52
Chapter Twelve: Unanswered Prayer 55
Chapter Thirteen: And Home Sweet Home (Not House) Number Three . . . 59
Chapter Fourteen: The Camping Experience 63
Chapter Fifteen: Forgiveness 68
Chapter Sixteen: Camping, One Step Removed 73
Chapter Seventeen: Taming The Tongue 78
Chapter Eighteen: Getting To Know Mother 81
Chapter Nineteen: Nostalgia 86
Chapter Twenty: Shaken Faith 91
Chapter Twenty-One: Finally Home Sweet Home Number Four 94
Chapter Twenty-Two: Building The Ranch 97
Chapter Twenty-Three: The Dry Period 102
Chapter Twenty-Four: The "Real" Rodeo 106
Chapter Twenty-Five: The Taming Of The Shrew 109
Chapter Twenty-Six: Unconditional Love 130
Chapter Twenty-Seven: The Last Prayer 138
Chapter Twenty-Eight: Yea, Though I Walk 140
Chapter Twenty-Nine: He Didn't Take Her 145
Chapter Thirty: The Terrible Twos 149
Chapter Thirty-One: Singing 154
Chapter Thirty-Two: The Skeleton In The Closet 160
Chapter Thirty-Three: Unmet Desires And Special Gifts 169
Chapter Thirty-Four: More Emotional Turmoil 182
Chpater Thirty-Five: The Home Office 188

Chapter Thirty-Six: Depression And The Conversation..................193
Chapter Thirty-Seven: Building With A Better Purpose.................196
Chapter Thirty-Eight: Physical Attacks And Life Changes..............201
Chapter Thirty-Nine: New Direction....................................206
Chapter Forty: Yea, Though I Walk…Yet Again..........................210
Chapter Forty-One: The Straw That Broke The Camel's Back – Almost ...219
Chapter Forty-Two: You Be The One.....................................225
Chapter Forty-Three: The Ranch (And Me) In God's Hands...............230
Chapter Forty-Four: Afterglow...233
Epilogue..236

Chapter One

IN THE BEGINNING

Isaiah 54:4b: "For you will forget the shame of your youth." (NKJV)

"You were born in a chicken coop". I was in my early teens when those words were first spoken to me by a family friend, and they made me indignant! Where would anyone ever get an idea like that and what would ever be the purpose of making such a statement? I didn't remember (and still don't) much about the house in which I was born and lived the first eight years of my life, but I had seen pictures and it was a house! It was a small house but it was a house, nonetheless.

Angered by those words, I took the first opportunity to question my mother about them. I wanted to be armed with the "facts" to substantiate my denial: I was ready to set the record straight. Much to my dismay I discovered from that conversation, that, alas, it was true. It had been a chicken coop – remodeled to be sure with no resemblance left of its original purpose, but a chicken coop, none the less. With that revelation came stigma and shame attached to my upbringing.

I realize only as I am writing this, that our "house" was actually the chicken coop of the previous owner of the house where my friend Margie grew up. I often wondered why our houses were so close together. Apparently, that previous owner had sold the coop and a small plot of land to my parents and sold the house and yard separately. I have no idea the size of the lot my parents owned with that coop: It couldn't have been much. It didn't matter as we children had no noticeable boundaries. To us one property melted into the other. Back in the forties and fifties, and living a few miles from the nearest city, it was relatively safe from outside predators and traffic. So we had "the run of the neighborhood" in which to play; and we did.

Just a few yards from our house there was a steep hill. It fell away one hundred fifty feet or so to a small creek and then rose up the other side. It afforded us many hours of sled riding and skiing in the wintertime even though it took so much longer to get back up the hill than the quick trip down. Skiing was a little tricky as it was so steep and short. You barely got started before you abruptly hit the bottom with the front of your skis, but it was fun still.

Beyond the hill was a storybook small section of woods with large maple trees and a pond. Beyond the pond was then a little open area that continued up to the back of a large home/horse complex used in previous years for fox hunting events.

As one stood at the back lot the building looking at it there were apartments attached to the right and above the equine portion of the building. Most of the area between this place and my home was fenced in for pasture for the use of those running this fine estate.

Venturing near and discovering they had horses, I also met a girl, my age, whose name was Nancy. We were only about five years old. Nancy was to become one of my dearest life-long friends. From the moment I met her I spent countless hours with her, spending almost every day at her house. To reach her house by the road was over a one-half mile trip so I often took the short cut through the pasture. I don't even remember her ever being in my house. I had nothing to offer in compared to her living quarters. In telling her about this chapter she told me she remembers being in my house on several occasions. It was there, she said, that she was introduced to tea. My mother and Aunt Helen used to drink tea.

Nancy was privileged to live in this amazing place. It came about as her father managed the small horse farm for the proprietor. The place was called "Hunter's Lodge", and as mentioned previously, its purpose had been to host fox hunts in years gone by.

The building was a complex of three apartments - a large apartment on the ground level in which Nancy lived and two smaller ones above.

Her family's apartment was situated in the center of the building and had a closed-in veranda running in the shape of a question mark, almost three-fourths of the way around it. The floor of the veranda was terrazzo tile. The tile continued beyond the living area, into and through more than one utility room, past our playroom and to the hay mow – a large area where hay was kept for the horses below. The area also doubled as a ball room on occasion in the years when the facility had been a hub-bub of activity.

We kids all had steel-wheeled roller skates and we skated for hours on that tile, around the veranda, and through those rooms. It was a vast area for little kids to enjoy. Our playroom was off to the side of our skating area. It was small but afforded Nancy and I hours of fun as a station for our Animal Circus training sessions. We "trained" caterpillars, worms, centipedes, snakes, and anything else we could get our hands on.

Below the hay mow was the stable area. One could go through that hay mow and down some stairs straight into the stable without going outside. The stable area was as impressive as the upstairs with a huge round tack room that boasted an all-glass front. Never had I even dreamed of seeing such a thing outside of a picture in a book, let alone standing next to it! (We were not permitted to go in it.)-

The veranda, running on three sides of the apartment was lined with windows the entire way around. Through the windows on the north side, you could see a paddock just beyond the drive to the barn. The house was on a little knoll with the entrance we most often used at the road on one end; the road then sloping gently downhill. North from the house the yard dropped off in terraces down to the level of the barn and on to the paddock of split rail fencing for exercising the horses. What excitement this place was to a child from a little house with no animals.

In that paddock one day, I first laid eyes on a special horse. It was a mare who came from out west and was of exceptional breeding and conformation. I felt fortunate to be close enough to a family that could handle such an animal. She was one of the first high quality Quarter horses to be brought into this area and once again I almost felt I was living in a dream world. To add to the excitement, I discovered the mare was born the same year Nancy and I were. Her name was Sutherland's Miss Chicaro. Even the name sounded regal to me. I quickly fell in love with her and dreamed of someday owning a horse like her. It was just a dream, to be sure, but I so enjoyed daydreaming and would conjure up wonderful things I would have and do in life. The mare didn't belong to Nancy's father, but to a friend of his and alas, she wasn't there very long before being moved and later re-sold. I was brokenhearted as I knew I would never see her again. Still, I would picture that mare in my mind for years to come. Little did I know that many years later this very mare would re-enter my life and in a strange way have a dramatic effect on it.

Beyond the barn, away from the road, was a kennel for housing the hunting and farm dogs and beyond the kennel was a tractor path that led along the top of a gully, then sloped gently for a short time on up the other side of a hill to the back of the home in which the owners of Hunter's Lodge lived. Along that path Nancy and I spent hours riding ponies or walking to the little creek at the bottom of that gully. It was the same stream that ran by my house further south, but here it was a bit larger with lots of flat stones that were home to numerous crayfish – known as "crabs" to us. We called it our "crab creek" and do to this day.

As of this writing the same stretch where we played so much of the time is still there, much the same as it was so long ago although only about 350 feet of it is untouched by progress. Nancy and I were able to visit it together not too many years ago and reminisce about our wonderful times there.

I believe I could describe from memory almost every nook and cranny of that wonderful place where Nancy lived and I spent so much of my childhood, but I remember almost nothing of the house in which I was born and lived for the first eight plus years of my life. What a wonderful, fun filled early childhood Hunter's Lodge and surrounding area provided me.

Incredible as it was at Nancy's home, we found even more wonderful areas to explore and play in. Directly across the road from Hunter's Lodge was a large barn used for milking cows. The property included two houses for hired help as the main house was over a half-mile away. I don't recall the barn ever having cows in it – that was a bygone era for the owner by the time I came along. But it stood, mostly empty, with many wonderful play areas.

For a time, my Aunt Helen and Uncle Ray lived in one of those houses while my Uncle Ray worked for the owner caring for his horses. The horses were kept at the owner's house further down the road, so we didn't see much of them. On rare occasions we had opportunity to go to the owner's yard and play on the elaborate playground they had for their children which included a short roller coaster track that ran from a little hill down into the yard. It was quite extravagant for someone of my means. Rarely were we in the horse barn. We did, however, spend many hours in the cow barn across from the Lodge.

The barn had stanchions made of round metal bars for confining and separating the cows at milking time. We often pretended these dividers were horses and would mount up and ride with our imaginations through the Wild West, a place that seemed light years away to us at the time.

The hay loft above was especially alluring. It was huge, high, and supported by enormous beams. Many wonderful hours of play were spent there. When the barn was full of hay we could climb right to the top and walk across those beams. It amazes me to this day how one can walk on those beams with great stability and ease when the hay is stacked up to three feet below them. But when enough hay had been taken out to make that distance 12 feet or more, fear took the place of confidence and stability and one could be in grave danger of a fall. We tried our best to be careful and were fortunate to avoid serious injury, although on one occasion it came very close to being a tragic accident.

Nancy had a sister, Janet, just a year and a half younger than us who, to our consternation, often tagged along. One time Janet was up in the hay mow with us and fell, landing on an upright positioned hay fork in the hay below. It punctured her leg, and while it was a nasty wound, it was not life threatening. If she had fallen inches one way or the other, it may have pierced her vital organs with serious consequences. The incident raised fear in us and made us a lot more cautious.

Special fun for us was trying to catch pigeons in the hay loft. We loved all creatures (except spiders which make the skin on my head "crawl" even writing this). Having a pigeon to hold and to train would be a great treat: Yep, we had to catch a pigeon. It wasn't easy; they were very elusive and of course much quicker than we were, especially since they could fly! But we were crafty to be sure and not prone to giving up. One of us would be ready to make the capture and the other would throw their shoe at the birds hoping to hit one and cause it to fall to the hay momentarily. While it was not a sure thing and many misguided missiles were "fired", from time to time, it worked and we caught a few. We would hold and admire them for a time, but our parents always made us let them go.

Behind the main large barn away from the road, there was another small barn and an outside hog pen which housed some pretty large hogs at times. Nancy and I, along with our more adventurous companions, could be found in that pen on occasion trying to ride those hogs.

Beyond the hog barn a short distance was the family "dump" as they were referred to in those days. We would rummage through that heap often, searching for treasures. Many times we found things we were sure were valuable and would stash them away for future use. We never made a dime out of that practice, but we had fun while we were at it. We probably ended up rethrowing some valuable antiques away.

Not far from the barn was an area of woods probably about 10 acres in size. To kids that were between six and 11, that was big. Nancy and I, along with other friends, her sister, Janet, and my sister, Jean, and some of my cousins spent some fun times in those woods. We never roamed the entire area but we did have a path directly across from the Lodge paddock that took us deep into the heart of the woods. There, on top of a ravine, was a small cabin. We had heard it was a Boy Scout cabin but it seemed to always be vacant and in later years was actually falling apart.

Many fun and spooky times were spent there as we would let our imaginations run wild and concoct all sorts of scenarios of goings on in it. With fear and foreboding we would creep up on the place and eventually get up on the porch. Much more bravery was required to get us inside. After progressing in increments, we discovered that it wasn't too dangerous so then decided we needed to tackle the lower level. There was a set of stairs leading into what we considered a great abyss housing the great unknown. Our imaginations would tell us we were likely to find skeletons down there, probably tied to unsolved murders. We were scared to death of it but we had to know what the lower level held and we had to prove our bravery so all together several of us slowly and carefully began our descent.

On one particular occasion when we were at the cabin, we decided we needed to see what was below those stairs. Since my cousin, Jimmy, was the oldest and the 'man' in the group, we made the decision he should be the first to descend. He got almost to the bottom, panicked, and almost knocked us down the stairs as he fled by us running back up. He didn't stop until he was off the porch and just about out of the woods. We were so terrified we screamed and ran most of the way home. It was a very long time before we ventured even close to the cabin another time and I don't recall if we ever descended those steps again.

Hunter's Lodge was where I got my first chance to be around ponies. Nancy had a large brown and white pony that ran the pasture between the Lodge and my home: Her name was Judy. We constantly begged to ride her but the men were usually busy working and couldn't take time to get her out of the pasture for us. We were told to go get her and bring her in; if we did we could ride her: We got an old rope and were on our way! I remember exactly where she was standing when we finally found her. She was on the side by my home just outside the edge of the woods at the top of the hill.

We approached her with treats and put a rope around her neck to lead her back to the barn, but we decided to ride her back instead. I helped Nancy up and then she helped pull me up. We were both on her bareback. The next thing I remember is Nancy being dragged after we fell off as she didn't let go of the rope. I saw the hooves come down close enough to her head to step on her hair! Undaunted, we caught her again and led her to the barn where we got to ride with a saddle and bridle.

Nothing was more important in our lives than getting to ride a pony. Later two Shetland ponies were acquired, Domino and Champion, which we were able to ride more often as they were smaller, and we could get on them easier by ourselves. What fun we had. Life was pretty good.

Chapter Two

MOVING

Deuteronomy 31:8: "And the LORD, He is the One who goes before you. He will be with you. He will not leave you nor forsake you; do not fear nor be dismayed." (NKJV)

Progress rears its ugly head: The main highway out of the center of Erie was a windy road which had a dangerous curve in it. So many accidents occurred on that curve that those in authority felt it necessary to straighten the road. Upon investigation of the matter, it was further decided to relocate the road to save tearing down or moving several houses and uprooting the families living in them. It seemed more appropriate and financially feasible to move the road just far enough to avoid that situation. Moving it to the east a short distance would solve the problem and require only one home to be destroyed – ours. Our home was right in the path of the proposed highway and had to be removed. It made perfect sense. What could be the significance of moving a chicken coop compared to several "real" houses?

The move came when I was eight and a half – but fortunately for me it was only a short distance away. My parents purchased an eight-acre tract of land a mile south of the old house and began to build a new house on it. With that chicken coop the first house my parents ever owned, I can imagine the excitement they (mother, especially) must have experienced at the thought of building a brand new, much larger, home. They built without benefit of a mortgage and did the work themselves, thus progress was slow. My two older brothers, Jim and Tom, were old enough at this time to be of great help in the project and worked many hours with our parents.

The basement was finished, and they continued to work on the rest of the house. We moved upstairs one room at a time as it was completed. After the little house we came from, this one seemed so big! It was ranch style and seemed to stretch on forever. It had three bedrooms, although only one bathroom. It still seemed plenty big enough to raise the five kids in the family at that time; the sixth one coming several years after we moved in. Having a full basement meant twice the room. I used to "camp out" in the basement from time to time and while it most often scared me, there are certain sounds I hear today that remind me of those days in a good way.

The move did not create too great a problem for me as I could walk that mile quickly and did countless times going back to Nancy's house. Things went fairly well, until when we were 11 years old, Nancy moved about 20 miles away. In those days that was a significant distance. My parents did not socialize with hers so there was no reason to make that trip other than for me, and that wasn't done very often. That move changed my life dramatically inasmuch as a huge chunk had been taken out of it. The Lodge where Nancy had lived, and I had spent so much time, was home to me and I so loved it. Now it was lost to me as well. Strangers lived there with no one my age. After Nancy moved, I never entered the doors of the Lodge again.

Nancy and I saw each other as often as possible but it was never enough. I was permitted to stay with her one summer while my parents went to York on vacation. It was so good to be with her. I remember going barefoot at least once during the week I was there. It is the only time in my life I can remember doing so.

Nancy joined girl scouts and as we did everything together, I wanted to join as well. Nancy came from a family of three children; I from six: My parents couldn't afford the uniform thus I was unable to join. It was an emotional loss for me and made me feel left out and alone.

Communication between Nancy and me was difficult as I was able to call her on the phone only occasionally because my parents could not afford the long -distance calls. I was lonely and I missed her terribly. Not only had she been the most important person in my life, her parents were like my own to me. I was especially fond of her father, Ray. He was a kind, gentle, soft-spoken man, and while he was working doing other things at the Lodge, he was a talented saddle maker as well. He made other things with leather and made two special treasures for me; a collar for one of my dogs and a leather belt I still have to this day. Many years later, just a short time before he died, Ray told me he loved me. He had never done so before, but I had felt it. Hearing it meant a lot to me as I had always loved him too.

When we were 14 Nancy moved again, this time to Love Valley, North Carolina where her father took a job making saddles. The pain from losing her increased. The move might as well have been to the end of the earth. In those days that distance was about the same to me. I spent hours writing to her over the next years as it was far too expensive to make a phone call that far away. Visiting was not even a dream.

Some years later Hunter's Lodge burned to the ground. Once again, I felt a tremendous loss. It was like losing my very own home. I miss not having the opportunity of showing that place to my children and grandchildren and sharing with them its importance to me. Very few pictures were taken in those days and only a couple of them are available to give a glimpse of the wonders of that magnificent estate.

With no place to ride ponies anymore I began begging my parents for one of my own. I so desperately wanted to ride, but even more wanted just to have a pony to spend my time with. I missed Nancy so much and I so loved horses. I cared for dogs as well and with no pony to ride anymore, I filled some of the loneliness with a mixed breed dog that I loved with all my heart. We were incredibly close.

His name was Pal, and he was exactly that to me. A medium size dog with fawn colored long hair, a white collar, nose, legs, and tip of tail, he was beautiful to me. We were not permitted to have a dog in the house, so he lived on a chain when I wasn't at home. Each day he would watch for me to come home from school and our time together would begin. In the summer we were together constantly, and his unconditional love filled a huge void in my life.

Two years after losing access to all the lodge had to offer, my parents gave in to my constant pleading and finally agreed to let me have a pony. The revelation was bitter-sweet as there was a painful stipulation attached to it. My mother told me I was not permitted to have my dog *and* a pony, and I would have to give Pal up if I got the pony. As a thirteen-year-old I was torn between my love for my constant companion and the dream of a lifetime. How I agonized over mother's mandate and how I begged for it to be reversed: It was not to be. I had to make a choice. I decided I wanted a pony more than anything else and gave up my Pal. The eyes of that dog longing after me as I left him tied to a chain in the humane society haunt me to this very day. I have never gotten over losing him. I was to suffer that loss and many others in ways I never realized until I was much older.

I went to see "the" pony I wanted and potentially had the chance to acquire. He was five years old, 56 inches tall, coal black, and a bit on the wild side. The barn he was housed in was back in the neighborhood I spent those first eight plus years in next to the old windy road with the dangerous curve on it. He roamed a pasture attached to the barn that was several acres in size. From the barn the pasture inclined slightly downward for a couple hundred feet then rose quickly into a rugged large hill with scrub bushes dotting the side of it.

I was standing in his pasture down by the barn looking at him from below as he stood at the very top of that hill, the wind whipping his long mane away from his face, my heart pounding at his majestic beauty. He looked for all the world like a wild horse! I was enraptured with Walter Farley's Black Stallion series of books and daydreamed of having a similar relationship as Alec and "the Black". This was as close to that type of situation I would ever get I was sure, and I was savoring the moment.

Suddenly, the pony turned his gaze upon me. He looked only briefly and then began to descend the hill, running in my direction. Gaining speed, he headed straight for me never once wavering from his course. I ran to, and ducked under, the fence just as he slid to a stop on the other side of it half rearing and tossing his head. He would have run right over me! He was just like the Black! Undaunted, I wanted him more than ever.

After considerably more begging, my parents bought him for me. He came with problems: He was half broke and half wild. My Uncle Ray ironically now lived in a new little house built on the same property where I was born, right next to the new highway. Uncle Ray had worked around horses for many years even traveling with large hunter jumper stables to shows as their handler and groom. Earlier in his life he had lived in Canada in an area where the only transportation was by horse. He reminisced of how often he made the 30-mile trip to town by sleigh or wagon, sometimes just to socialize.

Uncle Ray used to tell me he forgot more about horses than I would ever know. I'm sure he was right. He now lived and worked close by and took the pony I called "Midnight" (his name had been Trigger, but that was Roy Roger's horse so that wouldn't work for me) to his house to ride for a little while before turning him over to me as he was concerned for my safety. He worked with the pony for a few weeks before he felt he was ready for me.

Finally, the day came when Midnight was brought to me to stay. When Uncle Ray rode him the mile up to our house for the first time, he almost didn't make it! Midnight was tricky and tough to ride. He came with a bridle – nothing more – we couldn't afford a saddle. I rode him bareback. He *was* tough! He knew a lot of dirty tricks and tried and got away with each at least one time with me. We would be running along when without warning he would just suddenly stop and put his head down to the ground. I went over his head a couple of times before figuring out how to recognize the signs that would indicate he might be thinking about doing that trick and learned how to stay on when he did. Another nasty stunt he pulled was to be running along and suddenly duck directly left or right. That too, got me off a few times until I learned how to handle it as well. He taught me more about riding and staying on than

20 years of instruction and riding time under disciplined situations could have, I'm sure.

For the next two years I spent virtually every free moment on the back of that pony. We ran the woods, the hills, the creeks, the roads – everywhere those four legs could carry me. He was the love of my life and filled a large emotional need at the time. My parents never had to tell me to take care of him and they never did it for me. Even carrying buckets of water from the creek, one hundred-fifty feet away, and up a steep hill to the barn before a water system was put in, brought no complaints from me. I was that happy to have my pony at last.

The family that my parents bought my pony from was related to us in a round-about way. My mother's brother, Bud, married this man's (Robert) sister, Millie. Due to their relationship, we shared family reunions and other family gatherings. Along with three other children, Robert and his wife, Jill, had a daughter, Bev, seven years my junior. She was also horse crazy and had a pony of her own. When she was a little older, she got her first horse – a half Arabian. For many years we spent hours riding together. A particular event that never has left my mind is an afternoon we rode to a spot in a field, dismounted, and lazily laid in the grass just talking about things. As we lay there, we talked about God and wondered a lot what He was like and what He was all about. He was never too far from our minds.

While I have been raising Quarter Horses all these years, Bev has had Arabians and is now breeding show quality Arabs. When I first started raising Saint Bernards Bev also got one. If we weren't riding, we could be found with our "saints". During one of those periods, I already had two little boys to take care of. Fortunately for me, her parents were nuts about my kids, so I was often able to leave the boys with them for short periods and enjoy these moments with Bev and the animals. She was almost like a little sister to me, and we got along fabulously. We were very close and remain that way today. Ironically, my own little sister, Kathy, even though closer in age to me than Bev, was an annoyance to me. She was obviously mother's favorite, and she was always wanting to take my pony and do things with him every chance she had. How dare she? He was mine! I gave up a lot to get him, I trained him, and she just wanted to use him as if he was hers. I didn't like it much.

Chapter Three

RIDING TIME AND PONY THERAPY

*Matthew 7:11: "If you, then, though you are evil, know how to **give** good **gifts** to your children, how much more will your Father in heaven **give** good **gifts** to those who ask him!" (NIV)*

Construction of Interstate 90 in our area was just beginning. It was to pass through the area between our old house, and where we now lived. Missing Nancy so and still missing my dog, I was delighted when I found a new friend, Shirley, who lived close by and also had a pony. We spent a lot of time riding together.

Shirley and I would ride up on the thruway site and watch as they were building the road. Often, we talked about throwing ourselves in front of one of the big earthmovers and ending our lives. For years I was to wonder why I would have had such thoughts. After all, I had my pony.

Life should have been as wonderful as could be. It was only many years later, through counseling of sorts, that I was to realize the devastating effects loss could have on a person. I had lost my best human friend, the place that was home to me, surrogate parents, and my best canine friend. Apparently, I was not dealing well with those losses.

On top of that, I felt out of place in my own home. I was "different" from the rest, both in terms of personality and a lack of shared interests. I loved the outdoors and animals. My sister, Jean, two years older and closest to me in age, had nothing to do with animals or anything else I liked. My older brothers, Tom, and Jim, had nothing to do with animals and little to do with me, period. I felt I didn't belong.

I used to question my mother as to whether I was adopted. But why a woman who had three children before me and would eventually have a total of six, would adopt one made no sense, I reasoned, but I felt out of place just the same. (There was no way I could have been adopted as I was born at home with relatives present.)

At this time, my little sister, Kathy, five-and one-half years younger than me was the apple of Mommy's eye. I just filled my loneliness with my pony. How thankful I was for him! In spite of the emotional turmoil that was a constant companion of mine, no teenager could have enjoyed the great outdoors any more than I did for those two years.

Down the back road and about half the distance between the old place and home I discovered a barn that had horses. It was owned by Elmo Kelly and became known as the "Double K Ranch." Not only did they have horses of their own, but they boarded horses for others and there were people there every evening, working with their horses, riding, or both. I began spending a lot of time there, finding companionship and riding partners. It did not matter what the weather was like, I rode every day. I can remember sleet stinging my cheeks as I would ride across an open field in a storm and the sound of the tiny snowballs of frozen snow on the road as they crunched and squealed under the horses' feet on extremely cold nights. I was always without a hat, and I didn't know that feet could sweat in boots in cold weather, causing further cold. I was always cold, but I had to ride.

I spent countless hours on my pony, and we did everything imaginable and possible together. Jumping was a passion of mine, and I used every opportunity to do so. I had trails in the woods where I piled limbs and logs to make a "jump" trail. What fun! When at home with only an open field and nothing to jump, I placed two folding chairs a few feet apart and put a broomstick between and on top of them and practiced jumping it.

Elmo Kelly liked to tell the story of how he almost had a heart attack when I came loping in the driveway at his stable, still bareback, and headed directly for the riding arena, fenced in with a four-rail board fence, never slowed down, and just jumped into the arena. He also used to tell me not to take people riding into the woods with me unless their horses were in excellent physical condition as I would kill them trying to keep up with me and Midnight.

On one occasion I was loping down the road and on into their driveway, unaware that the drive had just had six inches of fresh bank gravel placed on it. It had not been compacted and was soft. We turned the corner at a pretty fast run, hit that gravel and down the pony went into a summersault. Being bareback may have helped as it threw me beyond where he landed. I got up, wiped the dirt off Midnight and myself, climbed back up and went on.

Midnight could be relied upon to run either to Kelly's, or if headed the other direction, home. One evening, while still at Kelly's and facing home, one of the men took the bridle off my pony and slapped him on the rump. We headed for home at a rapid pace! By leaning forward and pushing on his cheek, I gradually got him to turn around and we loped back to the barn and retrieved my bridle.

It has been said that I was quite wild in my younger days. Unfortunately, "wild" means something different now than it did in those days and I find myself explaining that my wild days were days of wild actions with my pony. "Wild" could also describe my looks as I spent little time on combing my hair or being concerned about my apparel. A dear friend of ours, Biff, asked a question one day in front of several people who laugh about it yet today. He said to me, "Do you want to buy a chance on a comb?" It didn't even embarrass me too much. I had more important things to spend my time on than myself and my looks.

When I wasn't riding, I liked to watch certain TV shows. Those I watched were Roy Rogers, Gene Autry, The Lone Ranger, and other similar shows. I so envied these cowboys, their horses, and the country they got to ride in. I went through a period where I wanted a white stallion like the Lone Ranger's (always stallions as they were so much more impressive).

To emulate my hero's, I taught my pony to rear on command. Still bareback, I would ride to a high hill a mile and a half away from home that overlooked one of the main roads out of Erie. I would time it so traffic would be at its heaviest for the day as folks headed home from work. Riding to the top of the hill, I would repeatedly cue my pony to rear and I would wave as we were high in the air. Back at home, across the road from our house, was a small field and beyond the field were railroad tracks used frequently in those days by all types of trains, including passenger trains. I would ride up close to the tracks and perform the same stunt for their pleasure (actually more for mine). I would begin the rearing act at the beginning of the train for the sake of the engineer and would continue on through the end where someone was usually standing on the caboose.

I never had a dangerous moment – none that I recognized anyway – on that pony performing that trick, however, my little sister tried it on him once when I was not around and ended up in the hospital. She must have held onto the reins when he went up and pulled him over on herself. She could have been killed. Although I had been doing this act for years without incident, it was my fault she was hurt. I wasn't at home when I heard about it and was very fearful of ever going home again. At the time, apart from my fear, I was angry: my sister was riding *my* pony, doing things she shouldn't have been doing with him and I was the one in trouble. I wasn't too concerned about her being hurt, but I was fearful for her life.

I made a lot of new friends during my time spent at Kelly's; some who are great friends to this day. Riding was my life. It was through the associations at Kelly's that I was introduced to the world of showing horses and with help from the folks there, I went to my first show. I didn't know how to do anything but jump so that is the class I entered. I loved it and wanted more. My father put some four by eight sheets of plywood on the sides of his pickup truck so we could use it to haul my pony to some of the shows and I began going regularly.

The very first year I competed I won the summer series jumping competition with my pony while all our competitors were on horses. I had a saddle by this time, but it was a western saddle with a saddle horn and I was not comfortable enough with that to jump in it so I rode bareback in all the shows. At one point someone tried to get me disqualified because I didn't use a saddle, but when they checked the rule book there was no rule against it; In fact, it wasn't mentioned. I'm sure no thought was given to the fact that someone might actually try to do such a thing as jump a horse with no saddle.

In order to show in other classes at the horse shows a saddle was necessary and I began riding with mine more often. Once I began getting comfortable with using it more, many a trip to Kelly's was done with Midnight galloping down the road, me with my left knee twisted under the fender of the saddle, right leg out of the stirrup and my body dangling on his left side facing his rear, my left hand on the saddle horn, my right arm held out straight to the side in the "fender drag" or "Apache hideaway" as I was later to find out the tricks were called when rodeo trick riders performed them. Is it any wonder my daughter and granddaughter went on to become rodeo trick riders?

At the horse shows I met a boy whose name was Bob who was also showing his pony. We became friends and would ride together around the show grounds between classes. On one such occasion I noticed this tall good-looking cowboy and I felt an immediate attraction. I had no clue who he was other than he was a calf roper. I asked Bob if he knew him and discovered he was his brother. I also found out his name was Bill, and he was 19. I was just a 14-year-old nobody on a pony – he a champion calf roper. I confided in Bob how attracted I was to Bill, and he promptly told me frankly to forget it. Bill didn't date, he said, and in fact didn't even talk to girls. Many girls had tried to contact him and get him to take them out, but he wouldn't even take their phone calls. Even so I couldn't get him off my mind.

Chapter Four

THE DANCE

Psalm 103:5a: "Who satisfies your desires with good things…" (NIV)

Summer vacation ended – school started – fall was upon us. In November I turned 15 years old. I had never gotten any closer to Bill than my conversations with his brother about him, but now Bill was showing up at Kelly's barn down the road almost nightly, playing cards in the tack room down there with some of the other guys who frequented the place. I was still there every night and now had even more reason to hang around as I could expect him to be there too. I'm sure I did lots of immature things to try to get his attention, but I never noticed any of them being effective.

The months moved on without change in that situation: It was March, 1958. Our school was holding a Sadie Hawkins Day dance called "The Dog Patch Match" to be held March 29th. The purpose was for the girl to invite the boy of their choice. Several of my friends knew of my attraction for this roper though none had laid eyes on him. They encouraged me to ask him to go to the dance with me. I was too afraid of being turned

THE DANCE

down, I told them. I had never had an actual date before either, so I was quite nervous about the entire thing. I also had never been to a dance. Finally, at their urging, I agreed to give it a try. Then when the time came, I got cold feet and couldn't face the rejection Bob told me to expect. I was so sad. There seemed no way I would ever even talk to Bill.

The time for the dance approached. I had told the girls I was not going to ask Bill to go with me. Then I started thinking, "I told the girls I wasn't going to ask him. If I do ask him and he turns me down, they will never need to know my humiliation over his refusal." With that in mind, I mustered what little courage I had and made the phone call: Bob answered. He knew who I was as soon as we began talking. Yes, Bill was at home – yes, he would ask him to come to the phone, but he told me not to get my hopes up. I waited fearful, defeated, expecting the worst. I was flabbergasted when he came to the phone. I almost couldn't talk!

I explained the dance and asked if he would be interested in going. He immediately said yes. I gave him the particulars as to date and time and he said he would pick me up. I hung up the phone and sat in shock. It was really happening! He was going to go with me! I could hardly wait to get to school and tell my friends what had happened. Life was good.

The night of the dance finally arrived. Bill came to pick me up. There was one small wrinkle in his plans in that he was unable to get his father's car that night and had to ask a friend to drive us. Bill didn't have a vehicle of his own. It didn't matter. We were going out and that was the important part. Along with his friend John, who was the driver, was his cousin George.

They dropped us off at the school. They must have waited in the car or come back from wherever they went early as they were waiting for us when, due to the dance being extremely boring, we left early.

There wasn't much to do in that little town, so we decided to take a ride down to the popular roller-skating rink. Skating had been a passion of mine born from those days spent with skates strapped on traveling around the veranda at Nancy's house as a kid. We lived 10 miles from the rink but as teenagers my sister Jean and I would frequent the rink by catching a bus up at the highway a short distance from our house that ran past the roller rink in Waterford. We did this on a weekly basis, skating until the rink closed for the night. We always depended on some of the kids driving around to give us a ride home: They always did. Often, we supplied them with gas money for doing so: Sometimes as much as fifty cents or even a whole dollar! That probably came from Jean's babysitting money – I didn't have any way of getting any. Actually, I did have a babysitting job at a certain point in time. I hardly remember it as it was so awful.

This particular night Bill and I stayed at the rink for a little while talking to others and then prepared to go on home. A friend of mine needed a ride – we obliged. In the front of the car were John and George. In the back seat were Bill, Bernadette and me. John took a very long way home and I so enjoyed sitting next to Bill. What a rush; what a dream come true. Somewhere during that ride, he leaned over and kissed me. Wow! I could hardly contain myself with excitement. When we got to my house and Bill walked me to the door, he kissed me again and asked if I would go out with him again. You know what I said.

Bill asked me if I would mind double dating with his cousin George and his date the next weekend. I told him that would be fine and asked who the other girl was. He informed me it was someone George met in school, and I wouldn't know her. I pressed for her name. Her name was Virginia, and I was surprised to find she was the same one who grew up next to us on the other side of the freeway where I was born and was a very close friend of my sister Jean as they are the same age. Up until the time of our move due to the highway relocation our houses were only a few hundred feet apart. They went on to become married and are to this day, but that is their story.

Bill and I went out that next weekend and began to talk to each other when we were both at the barn down the road. Weekend dates soon turned into some during the week and then nightly and all weekends. More and more frequently I would go with his family to horse shows and rodeos. How exciting that was for a wanna-be cowgirl!

Bill worked before school in the mornings delivering milk for his father who had a milk processing business. He would then go to school and immediately after school, go back to work for his father in his landscaping business. After work he would come see me. He was busy! He didn't have money for a vehicle of his own so relied on whatever his father would allow him to use. His father had a gold Ford Fairlane, a fine car, which we were privileged to get to use on occasion, but most often it was not available to us.

His father also owned a two-ton dump truck he used for landscaping which with high sideboards put on it, doubled as the means by which they hauled their horses to rodeos and shows. We often had to use that truck for our dating transportation as well. One of our favorite places to go was the Super 19 drive-in theater. We often went in the dump truck and when doing so had to park in the very back of the parking lot so we wouldn't block others' view. If the dump truck wasn't available, we would use his father's milk truck for transportation. That wasn't too bad, except for the fact there was only one seat in the truck – the driver's seat. I had to sit next to Bill on an overturned milk crate that was not fastened to the floor. Many times, I would slide from one place to another around that truck while Bill was driving! It never bothered either of us. We were happy just to be together.

Chapter Five

CHILDHOOD ENDS – ABRUPTLY

> *Psalm 25:7: "Do not remember the sins of my youth or my transgressions." (NKJV)*

I don't know when the arguing and fighting between Bill and I began, but I know that each of us had a huge jealousy problem from the get-go. It makes me wonder where we both got such insecurity that one could not handle seeing the other associate with the opposite sex. My attention had to be on him; his on me. We fought so much about it and I got so angry that several times I broke off our relationship but it didn't last very long and I always let him talk me into coming back. I remember one time in particular word spread quickly that we were broken up (probably wasn't for more than two days) and an acquaintance of ours asked me to go out with him. I agreed to do so and set a date. Bill found out about it and begged me to take him back. Of course, I did and to this day I feel badly about breaking that date as I know it hurt the other fellow's feelings. I thought this other person was a nice guy but that was also part of the problem. If a guy was too nice and treated me with respect and kindness, I thought he was a sissy and a little weird. I would have been embarrassed to be with someone like that. Boy, did I have a lot to learn! Many years later, that would be one of my big problems with my husband – the fact that he didn't cherish me enough.

Bill was 19 and I was 15 when we began spending all our free time together. It was no surprise to many, I assume, that two years later when I was 17, I became pregnant and was married – in that order. I was totally unprepared for marriage or motherhood. At the time Bill and I made plans to marry, my sister, Jean, was engaged. In an effort to save work and money for our parents, we had a double wedding. It only made sense; one day, one expense for the church and the reception. The reception was held at our parent's house. It was a beautiful day.

in 1960, the 28th of May. The four of us actually went on our honeymoon together to Niagara Falls and a little beyond. When we returned, we all lived with my parents; Bill and I staying in my bedroom while Jean and Harold made an apartment out of the basement.

My making marriage plans was going to provide the excuse for my parents to officially take my pony from me and give him to my little sister, Kathy. He was all I had: I didn't have another horse. As Bill and I talked about getting married, he asked me if I wanted to make it official with an engagement ring. I told him I wasn't really interested in jewelry. Knowing of my intense love for horses, and likewise knowing I didn't have one of my own, he did something I never expected. Instead of the ring, Bill surprised me with a young buckskin stallion to signify his intentions of marriage. I was delighted as I felt it was much more valuable than a piece of jewelry. How special that was for me!

Riding was such an important part of my life I never stopped, even when pregnant – not for any of my pregnancies. The horse I was riding just a week and a half before my second son was born, actually tripped and fell into a ditch with me. Neither of us suffered any ill consequences from the incident although he was born a few days prior to my due date, which didn't bother me.

Pregnancies were hard on me emotionally, however, as I was humiliated by my mistake that became obvious to everyone as the child within me grew. I had such a distorted view of sex that each pregnancy was an embarrassment as people knew what we'd been doing in order for me to become pregnant. I cannot describe for you the shame it brought me. I was sure every time anyone looked at me, they were wagging their tongues and pointing their fingers at me for what I had done. This shame never left totally and never lessened until our daughter, the last born, was 17 and I told her the truth about it. I couldn't deal with the deception any longer and I feared the day she would find out from someone else. Upon telling her, she replied, "Mom, I've known for years. It's okay." I can't describe the relief that gave me mostly just to get it out in the open but also to find out she didn't hate me for it. Twenty-three years is a long time to carry that load.

Our second son was born while I was 18. I now had two children that were in diapers and needed constant attention. Cleaning cloth diapers was a thing I always despised doing with a passion. If disposable diapers were manufactured back then, they were certainly out of my reach financially.

I had never taken time to learn to cook as I didn't like anything that had to be done indoors and now I had to look out for a hungry man and two babies. I hated to sew (again too domestic for me) and felt I was no good at it but I had to spend much time sewing to have enough clothes for all of us to wear. Life was hard and I wasn't handling it well. All those wonderful carefree days as a child and early teenager were gone abruptly and I was miserable.

Chapter Six

CHILD REARING

Psalm 16:5c: "He guards all that is mine".
(TLB)

I left the bank drive-thru one afternoon and headed home. I only had the two boys, they being four and five years old at the time. The custom in those days was for the teller at the bank to send out little, round, lollipops for the children in the car with you. Not ever having had or heard of a problem with them, I had no worry about them.

Children were not required to be in car seats in those days. I don't know that they had been invented yet. There were no seat belts for adults likewise. The boys were in the back seat of the car for the four-mile trip home. Things were normal.

I don't recall if Randy alerted me or if I heard the initial choking, but I turned my head enough to see into the back seat to discover Scott, wide-eyed and unable to speak. The sucker had lodged in his throat! I was alone, scared to death, and knew I had little time to look for help. There was no training available to the general public in those days to help someone in a choking situation so I did the only thing I could think of. I was approaching a side road from the highway and turned in and jerked the car to a stop. Jumping out my door I opened the door to the back seat as quickly as I could and grabbed Scott. I immediately turned him upside down and began pounding on his back. I pounded for what seemed like an eternity until the sucker came bounding out, bouncing to rest on the ground. Scott began coughing and I began crying. To this day I think of that incident each time I pass that side road.

Another incident occurred one day while I was off grocery shopping with Jill Stewart (Bev's mother) as was my custom every Thursday. One of the highlights of shopping with her was that she took me out to lunch each and every week. It was a treat beyond description for two reasons: I had never eaten at a restaurant in all my years at home with my family and I hated to cook with a passion! The boys were at school for the day, Laura Lee with us. Bill was at work on a job somewhere.

Randy was nine years old and had been playing on the monkey bars at school when he apparently fell from the top of the bars. He landed over the bottom bar hitting it squarely over his abdomen. He was in immense pain and was taken to the school nurse for examination. She felt he should see a doctor so tried to contact me. Inasmuch as it was before cell phones were in use there was no way to do so and thus she used the secondary emergency contact, my mother. Normally my mother would have gone and gotten him and taken care of him until I could be reached, but she was bed-ridden with back problems and was unable to do so. She did, however, call Bill's sister-in-law, Shirley, who was able to track him down. Bill went to the school to get Randy.

Being in so much pain, Randy was making trips to the restroom to vomit. He was sent by himself practically crawling to get there. Bill arrived in his old pickup truck, picked Randy up and drove him to the doctor's office. Upon examination they sent him on to the hospital. It was mid-morning by this time; I had been located and taken to the hospital to be with Bill and Randy.

They began examining and running tests on Randy that mid-morning, but for some reason didn't have the information they needed until about 6:00 that evening. At that time they showed us X-rays they had taken of his abdomen and pointed out that upon impact one of his kidneys had been cut in half by one of his ribs. It never broke the rib, yet that rib acted like a knife making a clean cut right through the middle of the kidney. The doctor in charge told us they had no choice but to remove the kidney.

I had no experience with surgeries; they had seemed to take their time in making their diagnosis and had shown no real measure of concern since Randy had arrived and so I asked if they were going to do surgery that night or wait until morning when it might be easier for the staff. The doctor turned to me as if I had just grown another head and said, "if we wait until morning, he'll be dead!" I felt like a fool.

The kidney was removed, and recovery began. He had tubes through his nose to his stomach for days - they drove him nuts. He wasn't able to eat so was being fed intravenously. He now had more tubes in his arm making him even more uncomfortable. He was miserable and it was hard watching him go through all this suffering.

After about seven days of this, they said they were going to let him start eating some Jell-O and if he could keep it down, the tubes would be removed. He tried; it didn't go well, and the tubes were filled with matter as it was drawn from his stomach. When Bill and I left Randy that night to go home, I broke down for the first time, crying, and told Bill I couldn't take anymore of watching him struggle so.

When we arrived at the hospital the next morning, we found Randy, sitting up, with no tubes! In the middle of the night he apparently had ripped them out. By the time the nurses found out about it, the tubes had been out long enough without consequence, the decision was made to see if he could continue to do without them. He managed fine, was much brighter that day, and began eating and feeling much better. God heard and answered my prayer although I didn't acknowledge or give Him credit for it. A couple of days later Randy was released from the hospital.

Scott had some minor surgery when he was about four years old. He was denied breakfast which didn't sit well with him. Surgery went well, recovery was swift, and we were in the hallway waiting for him to return to his room. We saw them wheeling him down the hall, Scott sitting up on the bed. As soon as he saw me, he said, "I'm hungry!" He was up and going immediately.

Scott was the adventurous type, or should I say maybe a little more careless? He seemed to be always getting cut or scraped or in some way wounded. Many times I treated him at home as was the custom in our family. My aunt Millie who lived next door was a registered nurse while some of the other women in the family were nurse's aids, or had nursing experience, and still another who became an RN. Their knowledge saved a lot of doctor visits. There were the inevitable trips to the emergency room for stitches though.

Scott was not a good patient; he was quite difficult to hold down for the doctor to sew up a wound. His screams — not the screams of throwing a tantrum, but the screams of "you're killing me!" could be heard throughout the rooms. He would not hold still and on one occasion, the completely frustrated doctor actually put him in a strait jacket to keep him still enough to stitch the wound without Scott jerking the wounded body part out of his hands.

Laura Lee had a bad reaction to her first baby shots, was quite sick, and scared me to death. We got through it and from that point on she was able only to receive half the vaccine of a normal dose.

The year Laura Lee was born was a booming year for me with babies. Six weeks before she was born I was given a special black colt, then Laura Lee, and then a Saint Bernard (actually she was Randy's dog) gave me 18 puppies!

Eighteen puppies is an extraordinary amount of puppies for any breed and this was more astounding as Shanda was quite small for a Saint Bernard — more of a Collie size. Delivery went along normally for the first twelve puppies but then she got extremely tired and things became more difficult for her. I ended up having the last six delivered by caesarean. Only one puppy was lost in the delivery process, and that at the pet hospital. Due to Shanda's compromised physical condition after such an ordeal, she had to remain at the hospital while I took 17 little bundles of fur home with me.

Since bottle-feeding would be a never-ending job, I was shown how to tube feed them and went home with the supplies for doing so. Even with the speed tube feeding afforded over bottles, it was a time-consuming job. The puppies had to be fed every two hours around the clock and when I finished with the bunch of them, it allowed me only a little over an hour until I had to start again. I still had many other duties to perform.

All was going well until Laura Lee came down with a fever and needed more attention than usual. At the same time the puppies picked up a little infection that can be deadly to them and while I was concentrating on my daughter, the infection got a hold in the litter and I lost five of the puppies to it. It was a heartbreak, especially after all the work I'd put into them, but I had no choice. In the end I successfully raised 12 of the original litter.

The boys were 12 and 13 years old. We were away for a day with relatives. We were at a spot along the Allegheny River where they could play and swim. Adults and children alike were all in the water with the exception of me. I don't handle cold well and that river was cold! I was sitting on the bank watching them. The bank I was on was about 20 feet from the river and between me and the river the area was lined with large irregular shaped stones. I was actually in my bare feet to try to get some tan on them. It was okay to sit that way but I would never have gotten up and walked around in bare feet.

There was a large area on our side of the river that was calm and supported safe swimming and that is where they were enjoying the water. As I sat and watched them, I noticed Scott getting further into the center of the river than the rest, in water almost up to his neck, and I became apprehensive. I shouted for him to come back in closer to shore and he didn't move. I saw a look of panic in his eyes and the swift moving current right behind him. No one else saw him or his predicament and I knew I had to act fast. I jumped up, raced across those jagged stones, not feeling a thing, ran into that ice water, still not feeling a thing, and made my way to him just as he lost his footing and began to slip backwards into the current. I reached for his hand and caught him moments before he would have slipped away. I shudder to think of what the outcome would have been if that had happened.

I should have learned that bad things don't always happen to someone else.

Little did I know what the future held for me.

Chapter Seven

HOME SWEET HOME NUMBER TWO

Psalm 22:19: "But You, O Lord, do not be far from me; O My Strength, hasten to help me!" (NKJV)

We needed some place of our own to call home beyond a bedroom in my parent's home. Shortly after our marriage, Bill's father had purchased a small business from an individual in a small suburb of Erie. The purchase included a garage for equipment with a tiny apartment above. It became our living quarters for about a year. It was such a hard place to be emotionally, I can't even remember exactly how long we were there! I know we moved out in March but am not sure what month we moved in. I do know I was in that tiny place with two babies. Randy was born in October and Scott was born the following September. At one point during the stay in that apartment I thought I was pregnant yet again. I called the doctor and told him I was afraid and, "if I am, I will kill myself." I meant it. Obviously, I was not.

I had never been away from the country, and this was too close to the city for me! I had also never been away from my animals and that was awful to endure. I felt isolated and imprisoned. Every day I drove back to my parent's home where I kept the horses and spent the day with them and my family. I spent as little time in that apartment as possible and it showed. I was a terrible housekeeper. The apartment was too small to put anything away. I hated it and was seldom there.

I had a very poor relationship with my mother and father in-law. They were obvious in their disapproval of me although little was actually said about it. In defense of them, I'm sure they didn't see much in me to make their son happy. I'm certain under the circumstances they thought I would totally ruin his life. In the meantime, Bill worked long hours every day and often seven days a week. I'm sure he was as unhappy as I was, but it was impossible to tell: We never talked. We did fight a lot but never talked. It was in that tiny apartment where I was to make my first serious attempt at suicide. I really didn't want to kill myself, but I was so miserable there. I was desperate for attention and help from Bill and acceptance from his family. I got neither.

My Uncle Ray and Aunt Helen had built a cement block house on a piece of the eight acres my parents originally purchased and now lived on. They didn't need a big house anymore and we did so we purchased the house from them for $6,000.00. The house was 31 feet by 61 feet, two stories, and we were quite excited about it. I would be able to keep my horses at my mother's barn until we got a chance to build one of our own but now, she was only across the field from us. I was back in the country: I was home. How grateful I was for that.

In time we did put up a barn by buying some low-cost logs and hauling them to a local sawmill to be cut up for boards. That could be done quite inexpensively in those days and was the only way we could afford to build. We had our own dump trucks to haul with and while I was driving a tri-axle dump truck with a load of those logs I got pulled over by a state trooper for not having enough flags on the load to alert others to be cautious. He asked me to step out of the truck and almost fainted when he saw this five-foot two-inch woman with a belly so big she could hardly walk. I was hoping he'd take mercy on me due to it, but alas, he gave me a ticket anyway.

Along with building the barn, we put up a roping arena next to the house, put in a kennel for my Saint Bernards and Bill's hunting Beagles, and still had a large yard. The yard had some lilac bushes one of my mother's uncles had given her. They were special to me, moved with me, and have remained with me to this day. A weeping willow my uncle had planted was getting quite large by this time and I loved it. The yard was beautiful.

The only thing we didn't plan well for originally was a drive to the barn and I was left to carry 100-pound bags of horse and calf feed from the house, across the grass, and down to the barn on a regular basis. It was approximately 80 feet away and not too much of an ordeal except for when I was pregnant or had had surgery or was in bed with my back problems. I had to find an alternate way for those times. I did so by having one of my best friends, Biff, make a harness for my Saint Bernards, (which I still have some 50 plus years later). I then hooked up one of the Saints to a toboggan or sled and had him/her pull each bag to the barn - right in the door and to the bin. I then had only to get it up in the bin.

After we'd been there for about 12 years, we decided to add on, remodel, and cosmetically improve the looks of the painted cement blocks. We could not afford any new materials but were fortunate to find some used lumber and cement blocks from various locations, most of which were free. I spent countless hours removing nails from the lumber and knocking old mortar off the blocks so they could be re-used. With these materials and whatever volunteer help we could get from family and friends; we added a large garage with a family room above it. The room made use of the entire area as one single room sporting a fireplace on the end wall. This one room was larger than the entire apartment that we had spent that time in previously. I had long wanted a fireplace and couldn't wait to begin enjoying it. The two remaining walls not attached to the original house were lined with windows, the one side allowing us a clear view of the yard, barn, and beyond, the other looking over the road below to the fields and woods I loved so much. It was beautiful and oh, so comfortable. I loved it and enjoyed it immensely.

Bill and my father bricked the front of the house while a couple of friends of ours and I put siding on the rest of it and new shingles on the roof. My sister Kathy helped us put the siding on as I recall. Our great friend, Biff, did a lot of work laying cement blocks and building the garage. I did all the work to make the house the way I wanted it for years to come. Bill did the work to make it more sellable as he wanted to move. Neither of us knew what the other was thinking.

We spent 14 years in that house. The time spent there gave our children the opportunity of growing up close to many of their cousins. It gave me opportunity to spend many wonderful hours with my sisters as we raised our kids together. My sister Jean lived within 300 feet of us, and Kathy lived a mile down the road. With Kathy and I having the interest in horses, we became extremely close and did most things together. The place has many fond memories for all of us.

The only thing we could fault the place on was the lack of room for all we had. We had about seven horses, a dozen or so calves, a kennel full of Saint Bernards with a Beagle or two thrown in, along with some barn cats and raccoons from time to time, and it was all on one acre. We longed for more room.

Chapter Eight

THE RACE

Psalm 119:117a: "Hold me up, and I shall be safe." (NKJV)

The summer of the year I was 20 years old, my boys were two and three. With them at that age it afforded me time to ride more often. I left the kids with babysitters when I could afford to, and I rode. Bev's parents loved my boys and would watch them for a few hours at a time. When I couldn't leave them, I put them both on the saddle with me. As soon as they were old enough to sit by themselves, they went along on a pony I would keep control of by holding a lead rope from the pony to the horse I was riding.

My apparent riding abilities gained me the privilege of riding several different horses as my reputation for doing so and my circle of friends grew. One such horse was Hilltop Star, a stallion, and for a time I alone had free access to him. I trail rode him as much as possible and I really enjoyed the prestige of being trusted with such an animal.

One of the local fairs was on, and one of the attractions this particular year was a horse race. Dick Thayer, Star's owner, had asked me to ride the stallion in the race. I had always enjoyed anything fast and daring and this was right up my alley. While I did a lot of racing playing around in the fields sometimes by myself and sometimes with others, I had little opportunity to race in formal races or on an actual racetrack. I was so excited; I looked forward with eager anticipation to the big event. This was going to be fun!

I had a horse of my own to ride in the race, but it would be much more impressive to race a stallion, so I let a cousin ride my horse and I made plans to ride Star.

Bill had known for days that I had planned on riding in the race and never remarked about it, but as was often his custom, at the last minute – the morning of the race – he told me I was not to do it. I argued that Dick was counting on me, and I couldn't turn him down on such short notice. Bill left for work with me still trying to convince him I needed to ride in this race. He was so insistent I felt I had no choice but to obey.

Arriving at the racetrack, I found Dick and told him the news – I wouldn't be able to ride his horse that day. He told me I must and he all but begged: I relented. I figured I owed it to him, and Bill would have to understand. I'm sure my decision was made easier by the fact that I wanted to race so badly.

I wanted every advantage for the race so instead of using my western saddle I borrowed my mother's good English saddle. It came with a stern warning that nothing happens to it. With a bit of indignation, I assured her nothing would.

The starting line was opposite the grandstands on the one-half mile oval track.

We were to run a quarter of a mile which was standard in that most of us were on Quarter Horses. The finish line was directly in front of the grandstands.

A large group of us lined up, and the race began! I jumped to the lead from the beginning, gaining the coveted spot along the rail. Heading into the turn, and still in the lead, my excitement mounted as I heard the hooves pounding behind me. A short way into the turn I felt my saddle slip a slight bit to the inside. I thought that wasn't good, but I wasn't too worried about it, and I shifted my weight to the outside stirrup to straighten it up. When I did the saddle went way too far to the right which surprised me. I then shifted back to my left and again, it moved far too easily and much too far. Something was definitely, and seriously, wrong.

Being in the lead meant, obviously, the rest of the pack was behind me. I began to think about what was taking place and that inevitably I was headed for trouble. I couldn't figure out what possibly could be wrong and quite what to do about it. Looking at the ground to the left of me, I reasoned if I fell it would be on my left shoulder and something was likely to break. Bill would be furious! But more than my personal safety, I was concerned about my mother's saddle. I didn't want to hear about that.

As I thought about the inevitable, I was watching the rail on my left. At the far end of the turn I was approaching, there was an opening in that rail to the infield of the track. I determined I would likely fall in that area and at least miss slamming into the track fence. I also calculated I would fall off the track and so would not likely be run over. That, I figured, was one good thing about my predicament.

A decision had to be made and very quickly. While I did not know what was wrong, I had to do something, so I threw my arms around the neck of the stallion, removed my feet from the stirrups, and lifted my body. The saddle parted ways from me and the horse. In my mind at the time, I had this image of it slipping off his back and down his legs with the cinch (wide strap that holds the saddle on a horse) still intact. Of course, I did not think that would probably have tripped him and we would have had a real wreck. Now my fear was my mother's saddle being run over by the group of horses running behind us. I didn't realize at the time the cinch had broken, probably in the jump start, and I had run about three fourths of the race in a saddle that was not cinched.

That problem over, I put my attention back on the race. In my bewildering situation, I had lost precious time and was now second by a small margin. I tried to regain the lead position but had too little ground left on which to recover and finished the race in second place, riding bareback. Now the problem became stopping the adrenalin pumped stallion without benefits of stirrups to brace against and coax him to slow down. We ran over half of the track again until I was able to pull him to a stop.

Bill still reminds me of how I could have been hurt by disobeying him but now he tells the story with pride of his wife's accomplishment. Mother's saddle survived with few scrapes – she wasn't too miffed. I had the experience of a lifetime although I didn't like giving up the win!

Chapter Nine

LIFE – AND NEARLY DEATH

Job 10:12: "You have granted me life and favor, and Your carehas preserved my spirit." (NKJV)

I always hated being pregnant due to the stigma that I felt while in that condition as a teenager and I felt the same shame even when, over five years after we were married, I was excited about the child I was carrying. I planned that pregnancy to have the baby born in March so I could cover up my belly with warm bulky clothing over the winter. I totally expected to be able to choose exactly when the child would be born since I'd certainly never had a problem getting pregnant before. I had decided I wanted a boy as it would be easier to raise all of one sex, I reasoned. The baby was born August 6th – so much for planning. I had fully convinced myself I wanted a boy until I heard the doctor say, "It's a girl!" How thrilling those words were to hear and I knew at that moment that deep in my heart I had very much wanted a girl. I was just unwilling to admit it to myself out of fear of being disappointed.

She was such a joy! Of course, she was the most beautiful baby in the world. While I was still in the hospital with her (they made you stay three days at that time) there was a small fire on another floor. Someone stuck their head into my room, explain briefly what was happening, told me there was nothing to fear but to wait there until they came back, and closed the door to my room. I was not self-confident enough to question or disobey their orders. I waited.

While waiting I was amazed at the thoughts that flooded my mind. This child, this daughter of mine who had been in my life barely two days, was in a nursery down the hall. As my imagination ran rampant with possibilities, I prepared myself to do whatever was necessary for my baby's welfare. There was no way I would ever leave without that child, no matter what I was told! The bond I felt with that tiny little thing that had just come into my life was astounding. My concerns were thankfully unnecessary as the fire was contained and all was well.

It was hot that August. Laura Lee was about a week old. My parents were gone to York to visit relatives. I needed to be busy, and I had asked the doctor for permission to at least mow the lawn. He said I must wait two weeks before getting back to work. I had been used to all the barn, house, kennel, and yard chores, lifting and carrying 100-pound bags of feed on a regular basis. I was also used to hauling to the manure pile the byproducts of that feed from the other end of the animals that ingested it, and I was restless. There were too many things to do, and I certainly felt well enough to do them. But, easily intimidated, I followed orders, waited, and did little to nothing.

When Laura Lee was nine days old, I had a visit from a dear friend, Bev Heintz (Di'Carlo) whom I used to spend a lot of time riding with. She had come to see the baby. She was there for a short time and got up to leave. I walked her out to her car, and as I turned to go back into the house, I felt a small pain in the calf of my left leg. I didn't think much about it other than I must have twisted something without realizing it. I half-heartedly limped back to the house. It was mid-day. The pain didn't go away but wasn't too hard to put up with. I went to bed confident it would feel better in the morning. Laura Lee was in the baby crib right next to my side of our bed so that when she woke up in the night, I only had to sit up to lift her out of the crib to nurse her. Around 2:00 in the morning I awoke with intense pain in my left groin area. I couldn't for the life of me figure out what could be the matter. It really hurt! I couldn't even sit up enough to get Laura Lee out of the crib and had to have Bill get up and get her for me. He told me to call the doctor, but I was sure it was nothing serious and I didn't want to bother him in the middle of the night, so I didn't make the call.

In the morning, the pain was even more intense. After I promised Bill I would call the doctor as soon as the office opened, he went off to work. I was alone and having a hard time with the baby and boys with all the pain I was having. I called my aunt Helen who was more than happy to come help me out. I then waited for the doctor's office to open at 9:00 A.M. and called to see if they could tell me what could be wrong. The doctor I talked to told me it sounded like I had torn my Achilles tendon but to come on in at 10:00 A.M. and he would look at it. It's a good thing he did.

I had no way to get there. I was in no shape to drive; Bill was at work and couldn't be reached in time to take me. I called Bev Stewart. She was 16 years old and hadn't had her driver's license long, but she came and got me and drove me to the doctor's office. The doctor examined my left leg, the source of my pain. He was shocked at how swollen it was, the purple color it had become, and the very cold-to-the-touch condition of it. He ordered Bev to get me to the hospital immediately. He said he would call and have Erie's premier cardio/vascular surgeon, Dr. DiAngelo, waiting for me in the emergency room. We obeyed. I still had no clue what the problem was.

Dr. DiAngelo was indeed waiting and saw me without delay. He had no problem diagnosing the problem. He explained to me that I had blood clots in my leg, and they would have to be removed immediately. I told him that was fine and to please hurry up and get them out as I had to be home in a couple of hours to nurse my baby. He said not to worry; I didn't. I had no idea the serious nature of the condition I was in. He explained to me later that every vein, vessel, and artery in my leg was clogged with blood clots. He had gotten what he could out, which was an eight-ounce water glass full of clots, but he was unable to get them out of the vessels. They would make new avenues of travel, he explained. That condition has caused that leg to be an inch bigger around than the other to this day. I was unable to return home for ten days.

While I was in the hospital, I missed my baby terribly. My family, knowing how much I longed for her, got special permission to bring her to visit me. They weren't allowed to bring her to my room, but after being in the hospital close to a week, I was permitted to get into a wheelchair and go see her in the elevator area. She had been dressed in the pretty outfit my cousin Ron and his wife had given her that said, "Baby's first trip" on it. I had planned on dressing her in it to take her to her first doctor's appointment. Those that brought her to me thought they would be doing me a favor to put it on her. It didn't make me feel good, but rather the opposite. It seemed almost like she was someone else's baby – I had been with her just a little longer than I had now been without her; they brought her and took her away; they chose what she would wear. While I so appreciated the opportunity to see her, it was not comforting. In an effort to keep from hurting anyone, I never told any of them of my true feelings and the sadness putting that special outfit on her brought to me. They will discover it, if and when they read this book.

During my ten-day stay, I received anti-coagulant shots every four hours around the clock for that entire time and felt like the proverbial pin cushion. In administering the injections, they used all available areas in each arm, my back side, my hips, and the front of my legs (upper part) and then finished up in my abdomen. I left the hospital on oral anti-coagulants which I took for several months.

The doctor told me to take it easy of course, and I thought I did. A few days after being home, I developed another new intense pain in the same leg, this time down the leg a little farther. I couldn't walk at all on it; in fact, I couldn't even stand on it. As soon as I would stand the pain would rapidly increase, and it hurt too much to stand. My mother-in-law heard about it (I honestly don't remember if she was there, or I told her on the phone) and she told me to quit babying myself and just tough it out – I would just have to use it. My mother-in-law was a tough woman, not given to babying herself, and was probably speaking out of her own experiences. I have had several major surgeries performed on my body after which I used no pain medication whatsoever. I was not one to complain about pain unnecessarily. Her remark didn't do much for improving our relationship at the time.

Unable to deal with the pain, I called the doctor who advised me to go back to Dr. DiAngelo at the hospital and let him check me out. Doing so, he discovered I had a muscle hemorrhage in the large muscle of my upper leg. It was caused by overdoing. He advised me to stay off it and let it heal.

The leg healed and I was able to walk more on it but, as a result of all those clots and resulting surgery, it was painful for a very long time. It was especially difficult when walking up any kind of grade that required more effort in the process. It would burn like crazy! After some time, the pain turned to only a burning sensation in the leg which then subsided slowly over the next many years.

By the grace of God, I lived and by even more grace, walked normally again in time. I marvel yet at the gift of walking! I didn't give Him much credit at the time.

Just a few years later, while watering a horse over the strands of an electric fence, (brilliant, eh?) the horse brought his wet face down on the wire. It shocked him so that he reared straight up. In doing so, he brushed me with his shoulder and knocked me to the ground on my back. When he descended, he landed right on top of the front of that very leg and then, in his fear, he ran from the danger area, running right over me rolling me along the ground for several feet. Fortunately, (I think), we were on the edge of the manure pile and due to the soft ground beneath me, the leg didn't break, but it had quite a large dent in it and was very painful! My first immediate thought was "it's going to clot again" and I got to my mother's house where I could put my leg up (as I had learned a great deal about elevating that leg!) while she kept an eye on the kids and I called the doctor.

The good news was there were no clots and little danger of them from the location of the damage. The bad news was the nerves in the entire front and top of that leg were damaged severely. For months I couldn't wear jeans and could barely stand the touch of a silk slip against the leg. I had to wear skirts a lot (hard for me) and try to keep them away from my leg. To this day a piece of paper on top of that leg, over blue jeans, can be felt and causes pain. Apparently, this malady will remain with me until I die. I felt a bit like Paul when he asked the Lord more than once to take his affliction away. He chose not to do it for Paul – or me.

Chapter Ten

PRIORITIES

Matthew 6:33: "But seek ye first the kingdom of God." (NKJV)

Animals were always extremely important to me. I believe my love for them was largely due to the fact that the dogs loved me unconditionally and that was something I did not experience from anyone else. I so longed for acceptance and love, especially love not based on my behavior. Dogs did that for me. Their affection was apparent; their love evident no matter what I did or said to them. Ashamedly, I admit there were times I was not as patient with them as they deserved, and I often smacked or jerked them out of frustration with other things out of my control in my life. I did have a special relationship with my first pony – he was quite attached to me – but I don't believe love and devotion is the same between horse and man as with dog and man. Still, I needed both dog and horse to bestow my love upon, knowing I would not be subjected to the rejection I so feared.

My life was problematic. The early marriage, the children while so young, the rejection by my in-laws, the husband who was rarely home and wouldn't talk when he was, yet demanded my constant focus and attention, along with even more issues, caused me to turn my affection directly to my animals. I loved my children; I took good care of them, and they were extremely well behaved, but I was not as affectionate to them as I would have liked to have been and I was far too demanding and impatient. I was too rigid with them, requiring obedience above all and said and did things to them I am very ashamed of. I didn't know how to show affection to them. I had no love to give as I had none given to me and never saw it demonstrated, and thus no real understanding of love. Horses and dogs gave me the only pleasure I got during that period of my life, and they were my top priority. When things went wrong with Bill, his family, or related things, I would ride and for a time be able to get away from the pain of it all.

My love for horses resulted in discontentment with having only one horse; I had a desire to have a herd of them – specifically a herd of registered American Quarter Horses. I had previously had one or two – the first being the stallion Bill had bought me for an engagement present. He was gelded a couple of years after I got him so was of no use for a breeding program. Several years later he was sold as he didn't fit in with our program. I never really bonded with him either. The only other registered horse I'd had to that point was another gelding. Again, there was no future breeding there.

At this point in my life, I was trying to develop an understanding of God's workings in a person's life as I felt I wanted to do things God's way. God says in His word that He wants to give His children the desires of their hearts, so I was waiting for this greatest desire of mine to be fulfilled.

An opportunity presented itself to buy an older mare with questionable capability of becoming pregnant, but due to that obstacle, she was affordable to me: I wanted to give it a try. If she had a baby, I would be on my way. The most exciting thing about this opportunity was this was the very same mare I had seen as a child at Hunter's Lodge; Sutherland's Miss Chicaro! She was the same age as I and the chances of her ever having a foal were very slim, but I now had the chance to own her, and I don't think I would have passed that opportunity up for any reason! We purchased her and spent time and money hauling her to a stallion in another state to try to get her bred to no avail. As a last-ditch effort, we turned her out in the pasture with the stallion I had ridden in the race I wrote about earlier in this book to let nature take its course. I hoped and prayed for the best. The mating worked and she became pregnant. Four months into her pregnancy, she aborted: I was heartbroken. I turned her out with the stallion again and she conceived one last time. This time she carried the foal full-term and produced a coal black colt. I felt this would be my stallion prospect for sure. I felt God had come through and had given me my desire as this colt was exactly what I had been praying for.

I was twenty-three years old when the last of our three children was born. This colt was born just six weeks before our daughter. He was beautiful, and I knew I had been given the biggest desire of my heart! After all, he was a black-as-he-could-be stallion and that is exactly what I had asked for. I started thanking God and telling Him if he would make him of the quality necessary to justify being a breeding animal, I would even be willing to give him ten percent of all breeding fees I received for using him for that purpose. Wasn't that generous of me? I certainly thought so at the time. As mentioned, he was coal black; a color that probably should not have been produced from the cross of his parents. I considered that another gift from God and that was, yet another desire fulfilled.

I loved black horses and probably for prestigious reasons particularly wanted that black horse to be a stallion. Not everyone could properly handle and exhibit one and it would prove my horsemanship capabilities in a new way with me strutting around on a gorgeous black stallion. I was sure people would flock to my barn with their mares to breed to this fabulous animal. That dream was short lived; alas, he lacked the necessary conformation, and I made the wise decision to have him gelded. Before resorting to that act, I had asked God often to change things in the horse so it wouldn't be necessary. I reminded Him I would give him ten percent of all my stud fees and wondered how He could refuse such an offer. I also could not understand why He didn't love me enough to grant me this request. Yet even as a gelding, the horse remained the most important thing in my life.

While all this turmoil in my mind was going on my sister, Jean, began nagging me to attend church on a regular basis. I finally gave in and went for two reasons: One – guilt. My mother lived across an open field from me and could well see all I was doing. She attended the same church so obviously knew if I was there or not. Even married and on my own, I still tried to please her so she wouldn't be upset with me, and reason number two – to shut my sister up. Once in church I realized this was where I belonged and made the decision to go regularly. When I was committed to that, I began nagging Bill in an effort to get him to go with me: He refused. He was too tired, had something more important to do, or any number of excuses to stay home. It angered me and I thought about staying home until he decided to go with us, but I felt going to church was something I should do for myself and the children. Likely part of me just wouldn't give in to him either.

With that settled in my mind, each Sunday morning I got up and took care of the horses, calves, and dogs, got a baby and two little boys ready, and got off to Sunday school and church. As Bill tells the story now, he finally decided to go with us as he knew with my mouth that everyone in church knew where he was (in bed) and what I had to go through to get there without him. He went with me out of self-preservation to see what pride he might salvage. In any event his attendance allowed him to hear about, fully understand, and accept God's free gift of salvation through His son Jesus. This was even more significant due to circumstances he faced years before.

When we made wedding plans the pastor of my church at the time – the one who would marry us – said he would not be able to marry us if we were not both Christians. The Bible proclaims we should not be unequally yoked together and there are good reasons for that. Because he wanted to marry me, and also due to the fact that he really did not understand what the preacher was telling him, Bill declared himself to be a Christian at the time. The pastor married us believing that to be true. Bill did not even realize the true meaning or need until those many years later when he heard an evangelist explain it clearly.

Shortly after starting back to church, Jean invited me to a Bible Study. My first thought was: "ugh, boor-ring!" But as before, just to shut her up, I committed to going to one. I told her not to ask for more. I kept my word, and I went. I was amazed at how interesting, exciting, and informative it was! I was hooked from that very first study. From that point on I went to every study I could find and find the time to go to. I devoured the lessons learning much and wanting more. It wasn't long before I became a guide for Friendship Bible Coffees sponsored by Stonecroft Ministries. I didn't need to know a lot or study to guide them as all things were clearly written out and done in a format for all to learn together the truths of God's word. Bible studies were an extreme boost to my Christian life. Over the next many years, I not only went out of my home to guide studies but held some in my home as well. Each and every one was an enjoyable learning experience.

During this period of my life, I made a commitment to the Lord to try to find out what He wanted from me and to put Him first in my life. The months moved on and through Bible study I was growing in Him and learning to love Him more each day – beginning to allow Him to change my selfish desires and wishes. It was during this process that He made a most difficult request of me. I felt Him definitely asking me to give Him this special black horse He'd given to me. I promptly told him "NO", as he was too important to me. I was sure He would take him from me, and I wasn't ready to give him up.

God is so patient. He spent the next couple of months quietly making His request known to me on a daily basis. As I continued to study His Word, two things happened: I fell more in love with Jesus, and I began to trust Him more with my life. It finally came to the point where I, still somewhat reluctantly and with a hearty measure of fear, gave that horse completely to Him. I was sure that would be the end of the dreams and plans I'd had concerning this part of my life, but I could deny God no longer. I finally said to the Him, "Lord, he's yours. If You want him sold, send a buyer; if You want him dead, kill him." It was to be one of those two options I felt sure, but I couldn't take the struggle any longer and had to let go.

When I made that statement as a genuine commitment of my heart, surprisingly to me, I immediately found peace about the issue. It really didn't matter anymore. What relief I felt. I waited for the final outcome… Nothing happened.

In Bible studies I was learning about promises that God has given us in His word. I zeroed in on a couple that I felt could be very beneficial to me: Matthew 6:33: "But seek ye first the kingdom of God and His righteousness and all these things will be added onto you", and

Psalms 37:4 "Commit your ways to the Lord and He will give you the desires of your heart." I spoke to Him and told Him I was trying to do those very things and gave Him a list of my desires (just in case He didn't know them). We had need of some material things and I was looking for more success and recognition in barrel racing and like activities. I wanted to become a singer. Time went by and my desires were not forthcoming, and I asked Him why. I reminded Him of those verses and His promises and told Him He wasn't living up to His end of the bargain; still nothing changed. I was a bit perplexed.

During the period I was struggling with this I got a phone call from a cousin who lives in another part of the state. Her family was among my favorite relatives and I always admired the closeness to one another they demonstrated. In our conversation she told me of a problem that had developed that had devastating effects on all of them. The situation tore the family apart and reconciliation did not look promising. She asked me to pray for her and the situation which I assured her I would do. I didn't talk to her again for a couple of months. It was Christmas morning – the phone rang – it was Jeannie. She told me the reason for the call was to tell me the family had gotten together, talked things out, and were spending the holidays together. After a brief conversation and celebration with her, I hung up the phone. As I did, I suddenly realized this was a direct answer to prayer. What a revelation! With tears in my eyes, I whispered to my Lord, "now *that* was a blessing!" I began to see that day that blessings – and desires of the heart - run far deeper than my superficial wants and needs. While I still couldn't see or understand the entire concept, I was better able to wait on Him and accept what He gave me without being quite so obsessed with wanting more.

Life went on. I grew in the Lord, and there was a definite change in me. I had learned a valuable lesson in giving up that horse. In the first place, God didn't want my horse; He wanted my heart! In fact, that horse remained in our family until his death many years later. He was the horse people learned to rope calves on, the one they learned to run barrels on, many competing on him in those events. If someone wanted to show pleasure, he was the one they rode. If they just needed to learn how to ride, he was the one they learned on. He was there to teach our future son and daughters-in-law to ride and was even here for some of our grandchildren to enjoy. He did more for more people than any other horse we've ever owned. Most importantly, God had used him to show me that my priorities were way out of order. He helped me see I had a family to love more than I loved that horse; a Savior to love even more and to give more of my energies to. The affections of my heart needed to change – and slowly they did.

Over the next many years, I continued to grow in the Lord and marveled at the changes He made in my life, especially in the 'desire' part of it. I began to see the spiritual side of things instead of just the worldly and the importance of material things and recognition began to fade. The 'desire of my heart' more and more became to be in line with what the Master wanted me to be and to reach out to others in need. True blessings came when I saw evidence of His working in other's lives as well as my own.

Chapter Eleven

ANOTHER BRUSH WITH DEATH

Psalm 5:11: "But let all who take refuge in You be glad; let them ever sing for joy. Spread Your protection over them." (NIV)

I was quite close to my mother's brother, Bud. I lived right next door (the closest we have ever lived to anyone) and I did the bookkeeping for his chain of drive-in restaurants. He depended on me, and I believe I was one of his favorite people. Even so our conversations were limited to small talk or talk about his business — no more personal than that. While I knew him well, I knew little about his personal problems or concerns. We children knew little of our parents and family's feelings as there was never any conversation apart from parent to children, orders and instructions.

The exception to that situation was my two aunts, Helen (my mother's sister) and Millie (Bud's wife). Millie and I especially spent time together talking about many things. I probably learned more about the family through her than anyone else but that came years later. Thus, it was quite a surprise when I received a phone call one evening from her asking me for help. She quickly told me my uncle had taken a gun, had shut himself in the storage shed in their back yard, and threatened to kill himself. "Would I come talk to him", she wondered? She had also called her son, Ron, and he was on his way, but he lived over 10 miles away and would be 15 minutes getting there. Time was precious.

I told Bill about the call. He was reluctant to have me get involved in such a situation but gave me the okay to go see what I could do. The kids were already in bed and never knew I slipped out of the house.

I crossed the 40 or 50 feet to the back yard where I met my aunt. She told me he just said he couldn't take anymore and was going to end it all. He then retreated to the shed, would not come out and would not talk to or listen to her. She felt I probably had the best chance of anyone to get through to him. While talking would be hard enough, what do you say to someone about to shoot himself? No one ever knew when I was contemplating such things, thus no one ever spoke to me about it. I tried to think of what I would have liked them to say, had they tried. (Bill did find me one time with a gun but he didn't talk much about it.) I prayed as I headed for the only door to the shed. "Lord, help me with this. Tell me what to say and how to say it. Lord, please keep me safe."

Calling out my uncle's name, I asked him what the problem was. He told me just to go away and leave him alone; he was not coming out alive. I tried to reason with him for some time and appeared not to be gaining much ground so after praying again, I made a bold statement. "I'm going to come in there were I can talk to you face to face." He said: "Don't do it or I will shoot *you*."

I looked up to the bedroom window such a short distance away where my husband waited for me. I thought about my children just a room or two from him who had no idea what I was up to. I thought this could be it for me – I could die tonight. What would happen to them? No one but the few involved had any idea of the potential danger I was walking into.

I prayed some more and this time I got specific. I said, "Lord, if he dies tonight, he'll go to hell. Please don't let that happen. Even if he doesn't accept your Son tonight, if he will at some point in his life, please save him tonight from this fate. Keep me from harm and You bring him out of there safely. Please give me the assurance You will do this and the boldness to go through that door."

With that done, I felt reassured. I took a deep breath and announced again that I was coming in. The same reply was forthcoming, "Don't do it or I will shoot you." I glanced one last time at my home holding my family and turned the knob. He warned me again. I told him I was coming in, and through the door I went. It was dark, with only a small beam of light from the house seeping in through the open door but it was enough to allow me to see him sitting on a chair in the middle of the shed. He was holding the gun in his hands and had it pointed in my direction.

Things being as tense as they were at that moment, I am incapable of recalling our ensuing conversation but, thankfully, it was not long before he gave me the gun, left the shed, and went into the house. What a sigh of relief that drew out of me! What gratitude I felt for God keeping me alive! What a thrill to go home to my family. How grateful I was for God's grace and mercy.

My uncle lived for many years after that and while we never saw anything concrete or heard him say anything about placing his faith in Christ, we do have reason to hope that, on his own, he did make a commitment. I praise God for His protection of me and the additional years He's given me to serve Him.

Chapter Twelve

UNANSWERED PRAYER

Proverbs 16:25a: "There is a way that seems right to a man,..." (NKJV)

There was a popular Country Western song some years ago that told of an incident in a man's life when he prayed for something specific from God, didn't get it, and realized later he was very thankful he hadn't gotten what he asked for.

We have so many "wants" we think will make us happy that, we begin to feel they are necessities. We pray for something with all our might and feel let down by God when we don't get what we asked for. Many times, we later on find it may not have been the best thing for us, had we actually received what we prayed for.

"Grace" was just such an incident. Years before, when I wanted to start a herd of American Quarter Horses, the opportunity presented itself to buy a registered mare with two colts. One was a yearling, the other a weanling; they were full brothers. The owner was asking very little for them and even though we had no money to spare, I felt this was an answer from God and I wanted them – sight unseen! I felt it would be crazy to let the opportunity pass by.

The horses were approximately 35 miles away and while that isn't very far by today's standards, 40 years ago we didn't pick up and run quite as quickly as we do today. With Bill's work schedule (most daylight hours of every day of the week), he wouldn't take the time to go look at them with me. I can't say I took that very well. I got angry and hounded him to go until finally one Monday evening, we made the trip.

There were Grace and the two colts, all bays, (bays are a shade of brown on the bodies with black lower legs, black mane and tail – my least favorite color of a horse) standing in a pasture. At first sight I thought they were just fine. To be honest they weren't the best looking and not the best quality horses I'd seen but I wanted a mare to breed badly enough to overlook the less-than-desirable traits and got excited just looking at them. I was sure I had found something to get my breeding program started. It would take longer as this group had the two boys, but the mare would give me more babies and I would be on my way. We went to the house to find the owner and make a deal. Can you imagine the letdown I felt when he told me he had sold the trio the day before? I was furious with Bill! I had asked him to take me to see them for over three weeks; he did the day *after* they were sold! It was entirely his fault, and I was not about to get over it or let him forget it. I felt he ruined my chances to fulfill my dream. I was so sure it was his fault I never gave any thought to God having any part in it.

I stewed about this deal for months until a friend told us of an acquaintance of his who had a mare and her two fillies for sale. This time Bill went to look at them right away. I'm sure he didn't want to deal with my attitude if it didn't work out to my satisfaction. This was much the same situation as the other group; a mare with her yearling and weanling; only this time they were all girls. They were much better-quality animals than the other trio and even had what I considered a more desirable color than the first family of horses. This group had two palominos and a chestnut (a shade of red). I love palominos and because they are not common, finding two of them together was especially exciting.

The owner wanted more money for these than the other group we had looked at and we didn't have any more now than we did then, so I figured I was going to miss out on this deal too. This one would hurt even more, and I couldn't even blame Bill this time. I just had to accept the fact we couldn't afford them. I was elated at the possibility, literally standing before me, of my dream becoming a reality and devastated that it would not happen. Imagine my surprise and delight when we were told the owner of these horses was looking to get rid of them and replace them with some cattle. Would you believe we just happened to have a batch of roping calves we had raised that were now too big to rope and thus ready to sell? We made the trade!

That deal was the beginning of my breeding program. Over the years I had a total of 10 foals out of that mare, (five palominos) some of which were outstanding. One of them became the greatest barrel horse I've ever had. While it was 43 plus years ago when I acquired that mare along with her babies, I had a daughter of hers in my barn not too many years ago for breeding. I've bred over 50 foals from my own mares to date and many originate with that primary trio of horses.

This second group of horses was so superior to the first I would have been blind not to see the workings of God in the entire situation. I began to see I wouldn't lose out by waiting on Him to make the proper decisions for me. While I was able to begin to grasp that concept at this point, it was to become much more evident in the future.

Ironically, some year's later, one of Bill's cousins ended up with the original bay mare, Grace, that I had missed out on. They acquired her long after the two foals she had were gone to other owners. They had Grace for several years but did very little with her. Due to a situation that developed in their family, they couldn't keep her any longer and needed to find another home for her. *They gave her to me!* Years before I had wanted her so badly yet couldn't have her and now, she was mine free, no less. I could not figure out what God was trying to tell me in this: I was to find out.

I had the mare for a few years and regretted most every one of them. The mare had a permanent lameness that made her un-ridable. I was never able to get her pregnant, (she never had another foal after those two boys

I saw her with years before) although I spent a lot of time and money trying. She caused trouble in the pasture chasing other foals to the point that I believe she was responsible for two of them each sustaining a broken knee, one by falling into a ground hog hole, the other by getting tangled up in a fence. This resulted in considerably more expense and trouble trying to save them. While both lives were spared, they were terribly disfigured and mostly unusable for anything. (I've never had anything like this happen before or since.) Grace tore down fences and basically made life miserable for me. I finally had no choice but to take her to the horse auction and get her out of my life. I was thrilled to have her gone!

This incident taught me much about waiting on the Lord. Left alone we will often rush headlong into things thinking we are right only to get ourselves into a mess. I also learned that God can be trusted to provide for me in His time and in His way and that He gives the *best* gifts. This lesson was to be the basis for an ongoing relationship of building trust by allowing Him to make decisions for me. I am still building that trust.

Chapter Thirteen

AND HOME SWEET HOME (NOT HOUSE) NUMBER THREE

Genesis 13:17: "Arise, walk in the land through its length and its width, for I give it to you." (NKJV)

A year or so after we did all the remodeling work on the house, and were thoroughly enjoying the new family room, a friend of ours by the name of John began telling us about a piece of property he thought we should look at. With one thing and another we didn't get around to it for some time. In an effort to find more room we had looked at so many places that didn't pan out and thus had decided we were just going to give up and stay put. (We had almost purchased a little house on the main highway in the middle of a hill with a very tiny yard and no place to keep animals. That would have been a tragic mistake. What were we thinking?) I credit God for stopping that purchase which would have proven to be nothing but a disaster.

One Sunday afternoon we made plans to visit our friend Biff who lived farther out in the country. We loaded ponies into the trailer and took them along for the kids to ride so they would have something to do while we visited and headed out to his place. We made a stop on the way and happened upon John who promptly asked us if we had ever checked out the piece of property he'd been telling us about. We said no, but since we had no excuse, we decided we would pacify him by going to have a look. John had wanted to buy the place for himself but was unable to at the time and was sure it would work for us.

We dropped the kids and their ponies off at Biff's house and drove out even farther into the country looking for the place. Neither of us had ever been in that area before and it was a bit difficult to find. Once we did, one of the first impressions we got was how remote it was. It was a dreary, cool, April day and by this time light but steady rain was falling.

The only building on the property was a cement block barn that sat by the road. It was 36 feet wide and 102 feet long with a large hay loft above. The lower part of the barn was lined with window frames every six feet or so, but the glass had been knocked out by the large herd of cows using it for shelter as they ran the acreage surrounding it. The doors on either end were merely several boards hanging on what was left of the frame for each. They reminded me of the teeth on pumpkin faces.

The land was laid out basically in a square with the highest elevation and largest area of level land surrounding the barn. A short distance away from the road and barn the land gently rolled across fields to woods and swamp that covered the back one-fourth of the property. All of it was used for cow pasture. We decided to walk the terrain to see what it had to offer.

Starting out to the north we left the barn, crossed through the open field, then turned east toward the back of the property crossing more fields, on into the woods and to the back boundary as evidenced by a fence line. We then followed that fence through the woods to the south end of the property. It was a long walk, and the rain was beginning to soak us.

AND HOME SWEET HOME (NOT HOUSE) NUMBER THREE

When we came out of the woods on the southern end of the property, we cut kitty corner back across more open fields to get back to the barn and truck faster. As we approached the barn again walking through mud, holes made by the weight of cows on soft ground, rough, uneven terrain, and drizzling rain, I told Bill, "This is where I want to spend the rest of my life". He replied, "Me too." It was probably the first time we agreed on anything.

There was a realtor's sign at the front of the property from which I got the contact's name and phone number, planning to call for more information when we got back home. On the way I told Bill before I pursued purchasing the place he would have to understand that as excited as I was about the farm I did not want to move out there if the kids would have to change schools by doing so. I didn't feel too optimistic about it as we lived almost 18 miles away.

In my first conversation with the realtor, I discovered there were 155 acres that came with the property and the price was quite reasonable. The realtor told us he wasn't sure the property would still be available as the contract on it was to expire that week and the owners had pretty much decided not to renew it. The good news was that it was in the same school district – we currently lived almost on the northern border of that district and this property was the last place to the south in the same district. Also, I was far enough along in my walk with the Lord that I told Him if it wasn't what He wanted for us, then, as much as I did want it, I did not want Him to let us have it. I was wise enough to know that if we moved ahead of His will, it would never work out and could become an albatross. I was fearful of that. I was excited and nervous at the same time.

The realtor said he would talk to the owners (two brothers) to ascertain their plans for the property. I prayed. The realtor came back with the news that the brothers agreed to sell to us. While that was exciting, we still had a big problem; we had no money. We prayed more. I told the Lord He knew how much I wanted it, but that if it didn't have His blessing, I knew I was better off without it. I was trying to convince myself of the truth of that statement. Almost ashamedly we told the owners that we didn't have any money but we did have a house to sell. After revealing the truth to them they graciously offered to hold the property for us for six months with a $2,000.00 down payment to give us time to secure the balance. We were sure we could sell our house in that much time. In the meantime, the bank gave us a $2,000.00 note against it.

The year was 1973. October was approaching when we would have to come up with an additional $23,000.00 plus closing costs to complete the property purchase and we did not have it. Banks, not willing to give a loan on land without a house for collateral, made no exception in this case, but since we only owed a few thousand dollars on the house we were living in they agreed to use it for collateral. They gave us the money and we were able to buy our dream location.

Because we had done the extensive remodeling to our home and because it was located in a desirable country location, we had no doubt it would sell quickly. We reasoned we would build a new house at the farm and live our dream. A new house was something I had never even dreamed about yet now if we were to have a house on our property it would have to be new. It was an exciting prospect I looked forward to with eager anticipation.

Chapter Fourteen

THE CAMPING EXPERIENCE

Genesis 26:3a: "Dwell in this land, and I will be with you and bless you." (NKJV)

I marvel at the "rigs" people are using to transport their horses these days. It's common for people to travel long or short distances to competitions, lessons, or play days with a 24 foot or longer horse trailer loaded with all the conveniences imaginable for horses and a living area in the front of it for the owner's comfort. It's often pulled by something that cost more than our house. Many literally have all the conveniences of home as they travel.

We certainly started out on a much smaller scale. We began with a station wagon pulling a small, homemade wooden trailer. We ate our meals either in or next to that station wagon, slept, and lived in it with our two little boys, each weekend we were at a horse show or rodeo from the time they were babies. It really wasn't sufficient, so we were always on the lookout for something bigger and better.

Several years went by and Bill got a pickup truck for work. Now we began looking for a camper to put on it to live in on those weekends away from home. We eventually found one we could afford. It was nothing to brag about as far as looks were concerned that was for sure. It was made of wood, was very small, and had a low ceiling. It fit totally in the back of the pick-up truck. But in addition to providing a place to sleep in out of the rain and cold it had a small table we could eat at. It was a lot more than we were used to and we were grateful for it.

Not long after purchasing the camper, Bill, with the help of a friend made a steel two-horse trailer to replace the old wooden one-horse. Wow were we excited about that! (We were married 26 years before we ever bought our first trailer – a brand new stock trailer that we had until 2015. What a delight that was as well.)

Several years after building that horse trailer we purchased a brand-new truck camper with sinks and a toilet. Now that was an exciting move up the ladder! We thought we had the ultimate rig with which to travel to the rodeos. While this camper was much bigger and nicer than our original camper, it was still small by necessity to fit on the back of a truck. It was wonderful to have for a weekend, but I would not have believed you if you had told me I would live in that little thing someday.

Two years had passed since we had purchased the farm and put our home up for sale and it still had not sold. Due to the lack of space where we lived, we had moved some of the horses to the pasture on the new property. That meant I was now making a 34 plus mile round trip each day to check on them and feed any horses or cattle we might have in the barn for any reason. It was very time consuming.

One morning during this period I got a phone call from one of the neighbors by the farm. They informed me a dead horse had been found along the road and they thought perhaps it was one of ours. I hurriedly made the trip out to check on it, fearful of what I might find. I had to travel close to two miles beyond the farm before I found the horse in question. There he was, lying on the side of the road just as I had been told. One look relieved my fears of it being one of ours but I had no idea where he came from and never did find out who had owned and thus lost him. Since I was out that far, I drove back to the farm and got out of the truck. Standing in the driveway, looking all around me at the land

I already loved, I asked the Lord why He had me come all the way out there for nothing when I was so busy. It was the first time in my life I felt I almost heard Him speak out loud when He said to me: "I am going to give you all of this for your home". I was so excited. I wished someone had been with me to share it. I was sure if they had been, they would have heard it too – it was that real. I remembered that statement on many occasions when it looked like things might turn out otherwise. God has been so faithful to keep His promise.

Since the house wasn't selling and we wanted to be out at the farm so much, we took our camper off the pickup and parked it on its jack stands next to the barn. The location was chosen for two reasons – to run a phone line from the barn to keep track of business back in town and a hose to the two tiny sinks the camper housed so we would at least have cold running water.

There was not enough room for all of us to sleep inside so the boys' beds were put in the covered barn bridge that led to the hay mow of the barn. Laura Lee slept in the camper with her father and me. Apart from going back to the house for showers and church on Sunday, we did not leave the farm until the middle of December when doe season ended as four of the five of us hunted and it was great deer country.

My father built us an outhouse for use that summer and fall. I believe I have a mental block about it however as I am sure since I lived there for six months, I had to have used it but for the life of me I can't ever remember going through the door. It's not that I am a prude or above such circumstances; it's that spiders like to hang out in places like that and I don't "do" spiders! What I do remember about it is the incident with the duck.

We had a Muscovy duck we raised from a duckling. We gave him the very distinctive name of "Yeller". Yeller apparently didn't appreciate the fine upbringing we afforded him, or maybe we failed in that respect, but in either case he was nasty. It was obvious he didn't like anyone. Even though he apparently had a healthy respect for me, evidenced by the fact that he never attacked me, he particularly disliked Bill and had no noticeable respect for him.

Every time Bill got within 10 feet of the duck, Yeller would attack him. He would take flight with wings and beak flapping, legs reaching for Bill's legs, obviously attempting, and intending, to do him bodily harm. It got so frequent and annoying that; Bill got in the habit of carrying his calf rope with him for the predictable encounter. As the duck approached, Bill would rope him around the neck, draw the rope snug and suspend him in the air for a few moments until enough oxygen drained from his brain to make him woozy. He would then let him back down, remove the rope, and watch the duck waddle/stagger away. He was then safe from another encounter for a few hours.

One day after doing some work in a pasture down towards the woods I headed back for the barn and the camper. The outhouse was the first thing one would come upon from that direction, as it was between me and the barn. As I approached the top of the grade and moved closer to the outhouse and barn beyond, I saw the strangest thing taking place. The door of the outhouse was being flung open and slammed shut; open and shut, from the inside – repeatedly. I was baffled. Getting closer I noticed the duck on the outside of the outhouse door. Getting closer yet I was to discover that inside that door was my mother! She was trying to get out of the outhouse, but the duck would not let her. She was trying to slam him in the head with the door, but he kept ducking and she couldn't hit him! It was quite the sight – humorous, even, I thought. She didn't find it so.

I was always trying to do things to gain approval from my husband and one afternoon I stumbled on a good way to do it. I had made a practice of hitching Laura Lee's pony up to the cart we had for her and driving the ¼ mile down the road to the bus stop to pick the boys up from the school bus.

Laura Lee didn't ride the bus with them as she went to a different school and was picked up at a friend's house each day when Bill came home from work.

This particular afternoon it was almost time to go hitch up when Scott's Blue tick/ Beagle, Jenny, started running a rabbit. She ran it in circles repeatedly not too far from the camper and I got the idea to shoot it, dress it out, and fry it for dinner. I was annoyed that I had to take time to go get the boys and thought my plan would end there.

I hitched the pony, got the boys, and came back to find Jenny still running the rabbit. I got the shotgun out of the camper, waited for the dog to bring the rabbit back around again, shot the rabbit, cleaned it, and prepared it for dinner. I was so proud of myself and felt much like a pioneer must have. I was so pleased as Bill was impressed as well.

December came, doe season was over, and we headed back to the comforts of the big house for the rest of the winter. Although we hated to leave the farm, we were anxious for the room and luxuries going back provided.

Chapter Fifteen

FORGIVENESS

Matthew 6:15: "But if you do not forgive others their trespasses, your Father will not forgive your trespasses." (NKJV)

With two children born so quickly and no time or money for insurance, we started out well in the hole financially. We had to pay for all doctor and hospital care out of pocket. While it doesn't sound like much money now, the over $4,000.00 of hospital and doctor bills in less than a year was to keep us strapped for a very long time. We only paid $6,000.00 for our house and we were given 15 years to pay for it. The other debts needed to be paid at a much quicker rate.

Bill began working for his father in the landscaping business when he was barely 12 years old. When he was 21, his dad bought out a small excavating, grading, and dump trucking business. Even though they had this new line of work, they continued to do landscaping, snow plowing, and Christmas tree sales. Significant debt was incurred in expanding the business and only a short time after the expansion Bill, Sr. stepped down and one of Bill's brothers stepped in. Bill and his brother were to work together for approximately 15 years.

During the first three or four years the brothers worked together I kept all the books for the company as it was something I enjoyed and was good at. I also kept books for many years for my uncle who owned a chain of Dog 'N Suds Drive-In restaurants doing the individual store books as well as the corporate ones. For several years during that time, I was also the assistant to the veterinarian who owned the Glenwood Pet Hospital, my mother's cousin, Jack.

Bill's partner and brother married and began a family. His wife worked outside the home for a time and then chose to stay home with her children. With more time on her hands, she asked to keep the books for the company. Reluctant but without comment I agreed, as it seemed established in Bill's family that this sister-in-law was the right girl for the family, and I was pretty much the mistake. I had no doubt she was the better one for any job. I handed them over to her.

Things went along as would be expected with the occasional incident that somehow always managed to make me feel inferior. Things would be said or done concerning business or personal financial positions that seemed to always have a detrimental effect on me. Emotionally I felt alienated from, and betrayed by, the entire family. My self-esteem declined throughout the duration of this situation.

Money was very tight in those days. It was hard to make ends meet with the little salary the business could afford. We had been struggling to make it financially on $60.00 a week with two children, all that debt, and then a third child. Eventually our weekly income increased to $90.00, and it was a most welcome raise. Fifteen years after Bill was an owner in the business, we were making $120.00 a week. He was still working six and sometimes seven days a week for the most part but many weeks we got no pay, as each request for such was met with being told business needs must be met first and there was no money beyond that to give.

1976 came and things weren't much different than they had ever been. We had managed to do the remodeling on the house and were making payments on the new truck camper we had purchased a couple of years before – the same camper we had lived in for six months the previous summer. Money was really short this winter and spring as we hadn't gotten a single paycheck in almost three months. We were not in a position to handle this type of deficit and were really struggling.

Around the beginning of May of that year, Bill began showing interest in the office end of things. I had very little knowledge of the internal workings of the business since I no longer had access to the bookkeeping. I did work in the field driving tri-axles and hauling gravel on occasion but that was the extent of my involvement. Bill worked out in the field having nothing to do with the office. He now wanted to become more involved in that area and asked to see the financial records. While promises to present them were repeatedly made, they were never made available. Bill continued to press to see them. While he had ideas and questions about some business things neither of us expected what came to pass as a result of his inquiries.

Without warning, over Memorial Day weekend, all books and all control of the business passed onto us. In one day, his brother and sister-in-law completely dropped out of the picture. By the time the weekend was over we discovered the business was in deep financial trouble with many creditors and agencies hounding for immediate payment. How emotionally painful it became to answer the door, the phone, or open mail dreading the requests that I could expect to be bombarded with by doing so. Creditors didn't care that I had nothing to do with the present state of affairs and they could be ruthless.

Overnight, literally, it was as if this entire mess was *my* fault! It certainly became my responsibility as Bill was not prone to do office things and he now had to do the outside work two had done before. I was the only one of the four not previously active in the business and now I had to attempt to straighten out the entire mess or lose everything we had. The emotional trauma this created in me could not possibly be overstated. My nerves were shot. One day I had nothing more to worry about than my family's welfare, the care of my animals, and how to make it on little money. Now I had more responsibility than I knew existed to that point. I found myself very angry with my sister-in-law over this and related matters.

The partnership was subsequently dissolved over the next few months, bringing more work for me and fear of the future as well. Anger burned over the situation and I wanted some sort of retribution, but as a Christian growing in the Lord, I was becoming aware of the need to allow Him to lead and to make decisions for me. While contemplating how and when

I would seek some sort of satisfying revenge, the Lord spoke to me very clearly about the matter. He made it apparent to me I was to do nothing about it at all. What? Was I to just sit quietly and accept this mess and the extensive life changes it would make for me? My life changed overnight and would never be the same! Wasn't He interested in me and my pain? Didn't He care that I now had something I could go to my in-laws with that would make me look better in their eyes? I hadn't asked for any of this – it was dumped on me. I felt betrayed. "How unfair could God be", I wondered?

God performed a miracle. Not by taking away my pain, anger, or resentment. No, I wasn't ready for any of that. The miracle was in my mouth. He told me not to destroy anyone or any relationship over this situation but to leave it to Him to handle. It was so hard! I was sure in a short time though that He would cause something to happen that would take care of the retribution for me. After all, He says in His word that vengeance is His. It was not forthcoming. We struggled financially while they now prospered in a new business – a business financed by money we gave them as a settlement. I was exasperated.

As I cried out to the Lord to deliver me from the stigma this situation was causing me, He responded by encouraging my forgiveness for all that had been done to me. How could I ever do that? Didn't He understand the impact this had on me? He even knew ahead of time all the years this would haunt me and all the trouble that lay ahead for us in this flailing business. Didn't He care about me? Did He only care about the others? Oh, the struggle of it all.

Unfairness was such a big issue for me no matter who was involved or how large or small the incident, but this was indefensible and should be righted! God continually told me not to act on it but to leave it to Him. If I had seen some sign of those involved struggling it would have helped, but there was none. Additionally, things didn't change with my sister-in-law being the princess of Bill's family and me the less than desirable peasant. Yet, in spite of all, God said, "Forgive". With much reluctance I vowed to allow Him to show me how. What a long, hard process that was. The forgiveness that finally came, even in a small measure at first, took me nine long years to work out with the Lord.

Another area of forgiveness came when I was informed by a counselor of the need to forgive my mother. I hadn't even realized I had anything to forgive – the things I experienced with her were just a way of life – the only way of life I knew. He further explained my relationship with my mother had much to do with my relationship with my children, my husband, and my Lord and thus should be given much consideration. That concept came as a complete surprise to me. Up to this point I didn't know I could or should feel any differently about her. I didn't hate her – we got along quite well in fact. But he was talking about something deeper.

While I couldn't put my finger on any specific incidents to attach forgiveness to, as the Lord directed my thoughts toward the issues, I did discover an over-all disillusionment and deep-seated hurt over many things she'd done or not done over the years. Even as I write I'm sure one such issue was making me give that dog up all those years before. That and the void of expressed love and concern did leave scars (and maybe some unhealed wounds) in my heart and emotions. I just never acknowledged them before. I didn't think it was important and never gave thought to them being rectified; they were long over.

I believe God allowed me to see my mother through His eyes. I saw a woman who had grown up with many pains and disappointments; a woman who carried many a burden not meant to be carried alone. I saw a woman who did her best, in spite of her upbringing. I saw a woman who needed love and forgiveness as we all do. I began to feel privileged to be the one to show her some of God's love and forgiveness. I hope it made a difference for her. It did for me.

Chapter Sixteen

CAMPING, ONE STEP REMOVED

Genesis 28:15: "Behold, I am with you and will keep you wherever you go…" (NKJV)

With winter over and spring upon us we were itching to get back to the farm. Due to lack of buyers for the house we had decided to rent it to a relative who was looking for a place to live where he could also keep his horses. He later asked to rent it for two years and then purchase it. It seemed like the perfect answer and so we agreed. Rent is probably not the right word to use here, since he planned on purchasing the house, we didn't even charge him rent. All we asked was for him to pay his own utilities.

In order to have more room than the camper to live in at the farm we bought an old, small trailer from my uncle Bud. (One thing Bill and I had both insisted upon was that no matter what, after living in a big house, we would *never* live in a trailer. It would be just too small we had always insisted, but after living in the camper, it seemed pretty spacious.)

It wasn't much but it was all we could afford, and it meant we could finally stay permanently at our dream location.

We moved the trailer to the farm and set it up on one of the highest elevations in Erie County, facing the west. In July of 1976 we moved into it. We had no wind breaks up on that hill and spent the next two winters there – the worst two winters in Erie history up to that point.

The trailer was not large enough for all of us with just two small bedrooms so we put a makeshift small shed next to it and attached a very small construction trailer to the other end of the shed. That construction trailer would serve as a bedroom for the boys and the shed between would house our barn clothes and other things of necessity that would not fit in the trailer. There was no heat in the shed, and we learned with the first cold weather that pop bottles (glass in those days) would shatter, noisily, when frozen.

One good point with little room in the trailer, housekeeping was at a minimum although storage was a big problem. We used the huge hay loft in the barn to solve many storage issues.

Our septic tank was a 55-gallon drum that was filled to capacity by the second year. It was evident to all in view of the back "yard" whenever someone flushed the toilet as it bubbled up and out onto the ground.

It was so cold in that trailer. The furnace would run continually in cold weather and not heat it above 59 degrees. I can survive in our house with a turtleneck and a sweatshirt at 72 degrees but anything less than 80 degrees is quite cool to me. It was most unpleasant trying to survive in that cold and definitely the most difficult physical part of the entire experience. With the other comforts I'd given up in that big cozy house with the huge family room and fireplace, this was difficult to bear, yet I loved the rest of the farm enough that it made up for some of the discomfort.

It must be said that our children were troopers throughout this entire transitional period. I don't remember them ever complaining about their living conditions or the gross inconveniences they put up with.

Due to it being so cold in the trailer, we went to bed very early each evening after dinner and chores were finished as each of us had an electric blanket. One night, lying in bed and before falling asleep, I smelled smoke. That in itself is unusual for me as I do not have a good sense of smell, probably due in part to having broken my nose so many times (eight as of this writing). I looked down toward my feet and saw a little puff of smoke coming up from the center of the blanket. Our electric blanket was about to catch on fire! That could have been another chapter, another story, or no written story at all.

The kitchen in the trailer was on one end with three walls of it exposed to the outside, two of them containing windows. Whenever it was cold at all the water in that end of the trailer froze. It froze on a daily basis all winter long. I was grateful that it did not freeze in the bathroom in the back of the trailer, and we were able to shower and do dishes in the bathtub. Laura Lee reminds me that she believes *she* primarily did dishes in the bathtub.

The stove in the trailer didn't work so we compensated by using a two-burner hot plate, an electric frying pan, and a new micro-wave. One of the first things I tried to use the microwave for was to bake a cake. That went very poorly. My husband doesn't appreciate microwaves yet today and I have never tried to bake another cake in one.

I was so cold the first winter that I coerced Bill into putting a wood stove in that tinder box for the next winter. I'm sure part of his reason for complying was that he knew how miserable I was in the cold, but the biggest reason was probably to shut me up. I would put enough wood in that stove to get the interior temperature up to 90 degrees or hotter. Why the trailer didn't burn down is known only to God.

It was so drafty in the trailer that I was able to hang items in the living room and they would gently blow dry. I had to hang things from time to time as the entire two years we lived in the trailer the clothes drier did not work. I had begged and threatened Bill in an effort to get it fixed as I hated going to a Laundromat on top of everything else I had to do. At a Laundromat one day I left some clothes unattended in one of the driers for five minutes and had several pairs of Levis stolen. What a costly deal that was! Bill's answer to my repeated "requests" to repair the drier was always that he didn't have enough time and we couldn't afford the parts.

As the years in the trailer drew to a close, a friend talked Bill into looking into fixing it, and fix it they did. The bottom line was it took $14.00 in parts and one hour to fix a drier I had gone without for two years. I was not happy and, of course, Bill knew it.

The vehicles were parked facing the trailer on that kitchen end: The door was on the side of the trailer. One cold January day I was heading out for a Bible Study, but due to the cold, I went out and started the car to let it warm up before leaving. I went back into the trailer to do some things while I waited. After ten minutes or so I picked up my purse and Bible and went out the door. As I did, I noticed flames coming from the front of the trailer. The car was on fire. That was bad enough but parked right next to the car was my first ever brand-new cowboy pickup truck. I was horrified. I was alone – no help around.

I thought briefly, "Do you risk your life to save a truck?" I immediately answered myself with, "You bet I do!" In those days we left our keys in our vehicles and I figured I'd be in and out so quickly I would avoid danger and I would also have a warm place to wait for the fire department. I ran to the truck, jumped in, and reached for the key only to find out the key was already on and the battery was dead. The boys were in the truck the night before listening to the radio and had left it that way. I had to hurry back out, run over to the barn, and call the fire department, waiting there in the frigid cold until they came and extinguished the fire. Fortunately nothing but the car burned up. Once again, I'm sure my family was well aware of my intense displeasure.

After living in the trailer for the first winter and half of the second, we approached the relative living in our house to see what his intentions about purchasing it were. He said he still wanted to buy it but had no money and wanted to continue to live there as he had been. We tried to explain we really didn't want to spend much longer in the trailer and asked him if he could even find a small amount of money for a down payment so we could begin the basement of the house. At least we would have something to look forward to.

Instead of trying to comply, he got angry, insisted he had no money and no way of getting any and, without warning, moved out. Only by chance (Divine appointment, I'm sure) did I stop by the house sometime later to find a termination notice on the door from the gas and electric companies. I was always thankful God pointed the situation out to me as just a few days more and we would have had a disaster. There was no basement in the house and all the pipes for water and heat were in the floor. They would have frozen and broken resulting in more than a mess. Of course, the renter moved his horses out as well, but not before they had chewed the wood in the barn so badly most of the stalls and any other areas they had been able to reach would have to be replaced.

It was just a short time after the house was vacant that we got a buyer and felt we were finally on our way. The paperwork was done and the date was set for the closing. Then, just a few days before that day arrived, this previous tenant went back into the house and trashed it out of spite. He had paid no rent for two years but had done some minor remodeling which was entirely his choice. He now wanted compensated for that remodeling. When we refused, he tore doors off their hinges, ripped up carpet, took down overhead lights, and left trash strewn all over the house.

By the time of the closing we had to credit the buyers with two thousand dollars to make up for the damages. It was money we sorely needed and was a tough pill to swallow. We had given a lot up to try to help this person and this was our thanks. Following God's leading and keeping the issue to ourselves, we told no one of the circumstances. Bill's mother obviously heard the "other side" of the story and concluded that it must have been something *we* did! It was hard to bear and difficult to put behind us.

At least, and at last, we were finished trying to take care of two places. Now we could concentrate on our new home.

Chapter Seventeen

Taming The Tongue

James 3:8: "But no man can tame the tongue. It is a restless evil, full of deadly poison." (NIV)

By the time we moved into the trailer I was a paradox of myriad emotions. I was thrilled to finally be at the farm full time, but I was angry and bitter as well. From that Memorial Day weekend on, life changed dramatically for me. One day I was a housewife with a part time job I worked on at home, a dog raising business, horses and related events to enjoy, and family all around me to spend time with; the next most of that was gone and I was responsible for a terrific mess. I was frightened at the prospect of Bill and I handling the business and all its concerns all on our own, already frazzled at the enormous legal and financial issues that were upon us, and frustrated that now I had to work every day all day and away from home at that.

Home wasn't the haven it should have been. With all the emotional turmoil I so needed a place to relax but home meant constant phone calls and many personal visits from somebody wanting money we didn't have. I lost any sense of value I might have had and it seemed no one cared anything about me as an individual.

Bill and I began to argue about the situation and the finances, and it always came back to my job to handle them both. There was a lot of resentment between us as neither knew how to meet the needs of the other. In previous years his parents had both said some very unkind things to me and made it clear they did not approve of me. Not once did he take my side or say anything to them about it. I struggled yet with that. I had nowhere to turn for outlet. He did not allow me to be on the phone with friends when he was home and made it clear he didn't want any of my friends here. Being away from my family and having no social contact with friends made me feel isolated and alone.

In an effort to let my family know how stressed, distressed, and irritated I was and to get them to understand the seriousness of my intent I began using stronger language for emphasis. While I did not use the Lord's name in vain, I used some choice swear words and I used them often. I was still a Christian and I was careful never to let anyone outside my immediate family hear me talk like that. I loved the Lord, I was attending Bible studies whenever possible; He was teaching me new things every day, and yet I allowed myself this disgusting practice. James 3: 10 tells us, "Out of the same mouth come praise and cursing. My brothers, this should not be." (NIV)

I was impatient with everyone – at least anyone with whom I dealt on a regular basis. I had a habit of treating others with a very patronizing tone most of the time. Things that now are so minor were big issues to me at that time in my life and I made big deals out of them. I was all situation oriented and not relationship oriented at all. If an incident happened with someone allowing something inappropriate to happen with one of my horses, I would yell and make a huge deal out of it, more concerned about the animal than the person involved. I was consumed with my needs and I nagged my husband mercilessly.

One major issue I had a very hard time dealing with was the way I watched Bill handle the boys. He said one thing to them and then changed his mind and held them responsible for whichever way he really did or did not say or mean it. He did it to me too. There was no way of doing it right and one would continually fail because of that impossibility. I would jump into the middle of most things with my mouth to try to get him to be fair to them and me. It did not work and generally only made things worse.

My eyes were opened to my poor behavior rather abruptly one day when Randy, then 17, took me aside and told me I looked like a witch to his friends and my mouth was filthy. I was astounded; here I was sticking up for them and looking out only for their interests. How could he think and say such a thing? Crushed beyond belief I did have the good sense to ask the Lord about it.

God confirmed what my son had said to be true. Regardless of what others did I was responsible for my attitude and actions. It was true that to my family I was a horrible example of the Christian I claimed to be. Once more I felt it was too big a job to make all the changes I needed to make and once again wondered if it was worth the effort.

With that exposure of my serious character flaws, I began asking the Lord if change was even possible and how to get out from under all these past mistakes. As I recall, the first thing He spoke to me about was patience; I'm sure that was because I had none. The least little irritation would make me so angry I would want to throw things. The only reason I didn't was I knew I would be the one to do the clean up when I was done. At least I was smart enough to know it would do no good.

One day while still living in that trailer I boldly asked God to teach me patience. Some of the methods He chose to use to do so are written in another chapter in this book but suffice to say it seemed every little thing that could annoy me happened and happened regularly. Some were much more painful and difficult than material annoyances.

Chapter Eighteen

GETTING TO KNOW MOTHER

> *Ephesians 6:2: "'Honor your father and mother' which is the first commandment with a promise." (NKJV)*

I had been raised in the church with my mother taking me there from the time I was days old. When I was about eight I asked Jesus into my heart as I feared hell. That was a good enough reason I felt at the time and the most I was able to understand. I learned a lot of Bible verses I've never forgotten and can still sing most of the hymns and choruses learned in that era by memory.

Home life consisted mostly of rules and "dos and don'ts", and I learned at an early age that it was far better for my health and well-being to try to be good. I tried to be good as I feared the consequences of being otherwise. The punishment for infractions often did not fit the crime and was often too harsh. Along with other types of punishment we got a good amount of tongue lashings and smacks across the face. Some were well deserved as when my mouth would spout things I knew I shouldn't say out loud to my mother's face or that she could hear behind her back. There was no discussion of a matter. Her word was law.

Other than this characteristic behavior I knew nothing about my mother. As a child I thought of her only as my mother, not a personality. I believe I was in my forties when my mother first told me she loved me and that was in response to my telling her first that I loved her. I'm sure she loved us all but was unable to express it. Raising six kids was a lot more work than it is now: That alone putting enough strain on her. I'm sure she had a lot of problems of her own to deal with as well. That became evident to me as I began to see her as an individual apart from being my mother. In spite of her short comings, I believe my mother did a better job of raising her children than the generation before her and that is commendable.

I have little doubt my mother had asked Jesus into her heart, but I saw minimal evidence of any commitment or surrender to the Lord, Himself. She was committed to church; she was committed to truth; she was always kind to people outside the family, but she was harsh with those close to her. For a time, I was very much like her. I realize now she had a lot of issues to deal with that she could not or would not turn to others for discussion or help with and I'm sure she felt God had let her down in many ways. With no example to follow I knew nothing about living as a Christian growing up, but I did have a strong sense of right and wrong and of being honest. I am grateful to her for that.

Having been reared to perform properly in order to stay out of trouble and hopefully be loved and accepted, I developed a performance-based lifestyle. Much of what I did in life and even later on for the Lord I did out of fear of reprisal if I didn't. That made it difficult to believe God simply loved me for who I was. In my early marriage I suffered with a lot of guilt as I was spending some Sundays at horse shows or rodeos instead of being in church and was afraid, once again, of the consequences. I even felt guilty knowing the 'work' I did for the Lord, teaching classes and the like, was being done out of fear of what might happen to me if I didn't do those things for Him that I *knew* were right.

While living in the house across the field from my mother I began raising and showing St. Bernard's. My mother got interested in the same hobby as well and joined me. She also became an important cog in the wheel of the Presque Isle Saint Bernard Club I founded, and we shared those many activities together. It was the first opportunity my mother had to pursue an interest apart from staying home and raising six children and I was happy to provide the outlet for her. We did many activities in the club including taking the dogs to the local orphanage and giving the resident children rides on sleds pulled by the gentle giants. Ironically, I believe it was the same building my father had lived in for a time, as an orphan, after the last of his parents died.

In time my mother and my father both got involved with the Erie Hunt & Saddle Club (neither rode) but made many friends within that organization. Previous to this neither did anything outside the home, so this was very good for them. I was beginning to get to know my mother a little bit away from the boot camp atmosphere I was raised in. It was good for all.

My parents spent almost every Sunday afternoon from the time I was little driving the countryside looking at farms for sale. My father always said he was going to buy one, but it never happened. When we moved to our farm, my parents were frequent visitors. They would bring their camping trailer out and park it there to spend time without driving back and forth. They both loved being there and I loved seeing them revel in life on the farm, something they always wanted.

Both my mother and father loved running the tractors and helping us make hay. It was great to have the help and fun to be a part of them having so much enjoyment. One did have to be steady on one's feet when father would start up or stop the procession when baling hay in the field, but we had many a good time. It was so good to get to know my parents and to see them as individuals.

I drove into Erie quite often for Bible studies and mother, while camping out with us, would most often go along. We spent a good deal of time together for many years. After I quit raising and showing dogs due to being so busy with the business, I did not have the time to spend with her as I had previously, and it was difficult for her. I know she missed our activities together; I did as well. After having looked at farms for years and doing nothing about any, Bill and I came to the realization that the fantasy my father was looking for was not the farm but the search itself. It became clear he wasn't going to take that leap and buy one. I wondered why but I feel it was out of fear of the huge commitment financially (although had they sold their house, they would likely have come out ahead financially after purchasing something this far out in the country) as well as the work an older place would need that held him back. By this time mother was approaching her 70s and father was well into them: Even though he'd never been ill, he felt he should live closer to hospitals.

Mother, however, wanted to be near the farm so badly she found two different small farms close by ours she wanted to purchase. One was about a half mile away, the other just over a mile. She was excited and having chosen the one just over a mile away, proceeded with the purchase. The day of the closing arrived, and my father backed out, refusing to move ahead with the sale. Mother was furious and never forgave him. She was to suffer two nervous breakdowns and two strokes in the years that followed, and I saw the anger, bitterness, and resentment toward her husband grow. Sadly, I don't believe it was ever resolved.

Watching this process was a great motivation for me to do whatever necessary to avoid the same relationship in my marriage. Initially I didn't realize I wasn't avoiding it, but rather following her example quite closely. It became not a matter of avoidance, but a matter of correction – much harder to do after emulating her for so long. It also became a matter of necessity if my marriage was to survive and to retain my health, but more importantly if I was ever to be of use to the Lord.

I am thankful to the Lord for His grace in making things different for me and my daughter as she grew up. Growing up as I did with little interaction with my mother, I'm not really sure how it happened, (and I certainly wasn't the best parent) but I enjoyed a great mother-daughter relationship with Laura Lee; she and I were very close.

Obviously, a great part of that relationship was due to the fact that I only had half the children my mother did to give my attention to and times were different now. Women did things outside the home. I only had one daughter. Laura Lee and I shared the same interest with horses and spent our time together with them. She was a bright light in my life, and still is and we shared many good times together. She was a joy and my constant companion until her marriage at the age of twenty-one. How hard it was to give her up!

I believe I was able to be that "bright light" for my mother for a period in her life and for that I am truly grateful to my Lord. She needed it.

Chapter Nineteen

NOSTALGIA

Ecclesiastes 12:1a: "Remember now your Creator in the days of your youth." (NKJV)

Certain sounds take me back to happy childhood days. The sound of a small airplane overhead gives me longing feelings of the first eight years of my life. My mother's two full brothers, Bud and Bobby, shared ownership of a small plane. Robert, (the person I got my first pony from) was one of their best friends and later became Bud's brother-in-law when Bud married Robert's sister.

Robert had an air strip and airplane hangar only a few hundred feet from our house. The boys flew their planes for fun much as those who drive ATVs today. It was their relaxation and enjoyment. The FAA wasn't so strict in those days giving them freedom to do some barn storming and other such antics with their planes. They did loops, stalls, etc. We could get a ride almost anytime we wanted one and we did often. We loved those kinds of things – what fun and fond memories. The noise of the planes flying was an often-heard sound and part of a slower pace of life. It now brings nostalgia.

My mother's aunt lived next to the runway and in the next three houses south of her, her three married daughters – my mother's cousins. My mother's brother, Bud, lived only a matter of a couple of hundred feet away from us in the other direction and even closer in that same direction, another aunt of my mother's. For a time my mother's father (the only grandparent I ever knew) lived just across a yard from us with his new family.

My grandmother on my mother's side had died years before I was born, and my grandfather remarried and had another five children. These children were close in age to me and my sibling's and grew up more as cousins than aunts and uncles. I grew up with family all around me. The only time things were different was when my Uncle Bud moved to Albuquerque for a short time. I had been very close to his son, my cousin Ron, in those days as he was closest to my age, and it was difficult being separated. I wanted so to go visit but there was no money to do so. He talked of horned toads that lived in that region and I wanted desperately to own one. I wanted to go get one or I wanted him to ship one to me. They were only gone a couple of years and moved back, much to my pleasure. I never got the horned toad....

When I was five years old, my Uncle Bobby took off in his plane with his best friend, also named Bobby, at the controls. They flew a short distance and landed the plane in a farm field and visited with friends. When they were leaving, something inexplicable. The plane made its ascent from the ground, made one circle of the field, and nosedived into the ground. Both men were killed instantly. Uncle Bobby was only twenty-six years old and had been my mother's favorite sibling. He was the youngest, and she had been like a mother to him ever since their mother had died. She took his death very hard, and I was to understand forty-five years later why she never seemed to get over it.

After my uncle Bobby died, things slowed down somewhat with the flying. My Uncle Bud quit altogether for quite some time after his brother was killed. Three years later we moved a mile south and were not around the planes nearly as often. Robert, who had flown fuel planes for the Army during World War II, continued to fly, however. His two sons still fly, giving instruction to others; one of them flies in stunt competitions and has done extremely well at it. Two of his daughters, while spending time behind the controls, never got their pilot's licenses.

Still drawn to the planes, in my late 20's, I took some flying lessons from Robert. One afternoon at the Erie Airport – as it was called back then – I was practicing take-offs and landings, when he informed me, I was ready to solo. After that I would take the written test and I would have my pilot's license. Thrilled at that possibility, I was at the same time petrified with fear, but he assured me I would do fine.

I was not afraid of flying alone. I felt confident to handle the plane. The written test would not be a problem; I was sure I could handle that. The thing I was afraid of was talking to the tower on the radio! I was too self-conscious to do it. Even though I couldn't see the person I would be talking to, I would feel like a fool trying to sound like I knew what I was doing. I didn't know how to handle the situation.

Just about the time I was to be left on my own to deal with it the weather changed dramatically, and it became too dangerous to fly. My solo flight was cancelled. I never went back. I was in small planes rarely after that and only as a passenger. I do miss flying at times and have many times regretted not getting my pilot's license. My brother, Tom has a small air strip that borders the back edge of our property and so the once often heard sounds of those small planes buzzing over head is heard again. Those sounds remind me of all those carefree childhood days.

Since this initial writing, my cousin, Ron, and his son purchased the property on our north border and have built an even larger air strip than my brothers. They have built a hanger and there is a lot of flying activity right next to us. Mark Stewart houses his stunt plane there for the summer months and can be seen most any good-weather day practicing dives, rolls, stalls, etc. in the sky above our ranch- talk about "full circle".

My sisters, Jean, and Kathy, and I had dish washing duties and none of us was happy about it. Many a fight and argument took place over the kitchen sink. We found many things or nothing to bicker about, likely none of them important. Somehow, though, through that process of being forced to work together we managed to find a mutual ground that could make the miserable task more bearable. We decided to sing together.

We sang a lot of different songs and choruses that we learned from various places, but for some reason, the song we sang most often was one entitled, "The Streamlined Cannonball." It may have been because we found it easy to harmonize with this particular one. That song brings back fond childhood memories – not of the dishes but of singing the song with my sisters. We had the special opportunity to sing it together not so long ago some 50 plus years having gone by since we sang it at that sink.

Many evenings after dishes were done, we gathered in the living room and practiced acrobatic moves. My mother had performed in her younger years as an acrobat and enjoyed teaching us some of the maneuvers. We also sang songs as a family around the piano. They were good times, but I have no concept of how long they lasted in terms of months or years.

Another sound that soothes me is the sound of buzzing bees. I spent many carefree days in my younger years in the grass and fields with my friends, and often alone, just enjoying being outdoors. I never went barefoot (a hang-up I still have) so didn't get the usual bee stings on my feet. I was rarely, if ever, stung so had no fear of bees. One of my favorite pastimes was catching honeybees by the wings and letting them stick their stingers into my pant cuff, rendering them harmless, and then letting them crawl around on my hands.

In my wistful teen-age years, I would scour the yard looking for four-leaf clovers. I tried to acquire some good luck by picking them. I found a couple five-leaf ones and a six-leaf clover once. Thinking of it now, I see the irony of finding all these good luck charms and storing them in my Bible, which is what I did.

Even the buzzing of flies, pesky as they are, takes my mind back to lazy childhood days when summers seemed endless and there was nothing better to do than ride a bike, climb a tree and read a book while there, build a "cabin" in the tall grass, or lie in the grass and look for forms in the clouds.

I hear the occasional whistle of a train when the wind is right as it travels on tracks almost three miles away and it reminds me of those fun-packed days when I would ride my pony to the tracks and show off for the passengers.

Life today is so far removed from those wonderful days, and I wonder how many children will have opportunity to experience things as we did when we grew up.

Chapter Twenty

SHAKEN FAITH

2 Corinthians 5:7: "For we walk by faith, not by sight." (NKJV)

My uncle Ray, who had ridden that first pony for me all those years earlier, had become very close to me as I was the one in the family with the most interest in horses, and horses were mostly what he cared about in life. After we bought our house from him, he moved into a very small trailer behind my parent's home just across the field from us. With his life-long interest in horses, he naturally migrated my way. Before he died, he gave me the one possession that meant something to him: a steel mane comb for horses. He told me not to stick it in a drawer but to use it. I'm sorry to say I didn't follow his instructions; the comb constituted this man's worldly goods. With children and others around the barn I was afraid it would get lost, and it meant a lot to both of us. It has remained in a drawer and is a fond memory of our relationship.

Knowing we were moving to the farm was a big concern for my uncle Ray. He cared a lot about me, and he was able to see the hard road ahead making something out of the place we bought. He was afraid I would work myself to death. I probably came close at times, but I love physical work, love the outdoors, and I often remembered his concerns as I went about the long task of renovation and building. How I wish he could see it (and me) today. We both survived quite well.

Not too long before we were to move, he was diagnosed with cancer and was dying. I read my Bible and I prayed for him. He had spent his life drinking and carousing, but I loved him and didn't want him to go to hell. As the disease progressed there was a change in his demeanor, and he said he had received Jesus as Savior. I was thrilled. Reading regularly in my Bible I came across a verse that made my heart light. I had no doubt God had directed me to it and intended for it to console me. It read: "…the purpose of this illness is not death". (LBT) I immediately thanked God that my uncle Ray was not going to die from this disease but would indeed survive it. I kept the revelation to myself and waited for his healing. However, his health did not improve; he wasted away and died, just a couple of months before we moved to the farm permanently. I was not only heartbroken to lose him, but my faith in God and His word was severely rocked. The very foundation of my Christianity was knocked loose. How could I be so wrong? How could God tell me this and not come through? I was so shaken I did not mention it to anyone as I didn't want them to know that God's word could not always be depended upon.

Years went by; I still read and basically believed my Bible. I still grew in the Lord – I was learning to love and trust Him more. He was doing things in my life that were undeniable, yet that unsettling incident with my Uncle Ray and God's broken promise would not leave me. How can I believe anything God says, (even though I've seen Him come through for me as promised in other areas), if He doesn't *always* do what He promises? I had this nagging sense of God not being as trustworthy as people taught. How do I deal with it? How can I lead Bible studies and teach others to trust, depend on, and turn to God in all situations when He so totally let me down in this one?

My struggle continued for many years. Throughout those years I would often ask the Lord, "why?" I got no answer. That, in itself, was disheartening and frightening.

It was over fifteen years after my uncle died, and once again, I was crying out to the Lord about this matter: This time He chose to reply. Finally, and obviously, the time had come when He felt I was ready for the answer, and He enabled me to see the truth. The truth was He had never lied to me, nor had He deceived me in any way: I simply hadn't understood what He was trying to tell me. I had so wanted my uncle to be healed, it was the only possibility I saw in the words the Lord had given me. Why God let me flounder for all that time without responding to me, I do not know, but He now revealed to me the truth of the situation and the purpose for leading me to that verse so long ago. My Uncle Ray had wanted no part of Jesus his entire life – not until he became sick and faced death. It was the illness that turned his thoughts and his heart toward God. Without that illness he may never have asked God to be with him, to save him, and take him to heaven. God didn't promise me something and then not make good on His promise. The purpose of his illness was *not* death – the purpose of his illness was to turn him to Jesus and give him eternal life! The *purpose* was realized! What a relief to my troubled soul to realize God does not lie no matter how it may seem to me at the time.

Chapter Twenty-One

FINALLY HOME SWEET HOME NUMBER FOUR

Deuteronomy 5:33: "You shall walk in all the ways which the Lord your God has commanded you, that you may live and that it may be well with you, and that you may prolong your days in the land which you shall possess." (NKJV)

After living in the camper, then the trailer, and putting up with the problems with the other house, building a new home was a much-anticipated event. We were always looking for ways to make it financially possible to afford the house we wanted. A big opportunity to do so came with the area of marketable trees on the property surrounding a gravel pit we owned. We had enough trees cut and sawed to provide all the framing lumber we needed.

With the contacts Bill had through the business, we were able to hire some brothers who were house builders to do the building, paying them by the hour instead of a flat rate. That saved thousands of dollars. Bill and I did what we could to keep costs down. I did all the wood finishing on the inside; doors, trim, cupboard doors and such and I painted and papered walls. Bill did the basement excavation, septic, and drainage work. My bother-in-law, Harold, built our kitchen cupboards and put the counter tops on. Bill, the kids, and I gathered rocks from the fields to use for building one of the fireplaces. All these undertakings resulted in a tremendous savings. When we were finished the house was worth three times what the house we left had been worth and we only had a small mortgage to pay off in the next 15 years. God did a great job in providing this home.

Once we moved into the house, and in addition to many things to be grateful for, one of the things I marveled at and thanked God for on a regular basis for over twenty-five years was the abundance of hot water we enjoyed. Every shower was a delight and an opportunity to be reminded of where we came from and the multiple blessings of God. It is something that 40 years later generates gratitude in me still as I shower and remember. It was wonderful to have ample room again, although I still missed (and still do!) that large family room from the previous house. It was somewhat made up for by the fact that we now have a large basement. We put a pool table and a ping pong table down there and they have given many hours of enjoyment to many people.

The children all missed the cousins they had grown up so close to. They had been a stone's throw away all their lives and we now lived in an area where our nearest neighbors were some distance away. The boys eventually found some friends within walking distance (a long walk) and when they and their friends from school reached driving age more of them were able to make the trip out here to our home.

Randy and Scott began having friends come out on a Friday and stay over with them. It was not unusual to have anywhere from two to six extra boys spending a weekend. I never knew how many there might be at any given time. One Sunday after church as I was preparing dinner for the five of us, friends began showing up at a rate that resulted in 17 of us sitting down to dinner. In time two of the boy's friends (brothers) moved in and lived with us until one went in the service and the other got married. They are still like sons to me.

Having struggled with so little for so long, I wanted the world to see my success with my new home. I went so far as to tell the Lord that I would be content to live even just five years in this new home before losing it for any reason. I selfishly wanted everyone to see all that God had given us and we had accomplished. My, did those five years ever fly by! I'm glad God didn't take me up on that selfish request. We have been in our home 39 years as of this writing and I have learned a lot about my vain desires in that grace period God has given me.

In moving into the house of my dreams in my dream location I also discovered a new home would not solve my problems nor make me happy. A change of environment can relieve many difficulties and can make life easier, but it doesn't magically change one's emotions or character. Circumstances outside the home likely exist just as before and while it is sometimes possible to change those, one's emotional make-up can take a much longer time to alter. Sometimes the two remain intertwined and change much slower and much harder than one would like or hope for: at least it was that way in my case.

Chapter Twenty-Two

BUILDING THE RANCH

Ecclesiastes 3:13: "And also that every man should eat and drink and enjoy the good of all his labor—it is the gift of God." (NKJV)

The long, hard process of building began. One hundred head of cattle had free access to the barn and the acreage for a considerable amount of time before we bought it so the first major project was one of cleaning up. One of the pieces of equipment we had for the business was a small dozer and using it on weekends, when not being used on a job, Bill started bulldozing the manure out of the barn. It resulted in a pile that took us five years to dispose of as we found the means. We had no way to spread the manure on the fields as we came out here with virtually no farming equipment and it would be many years until we had money available to purchase any. In the meantime, we learned to make do with what we had – not always an easy task.

With the nice mares we now owned, I began living my dream of raising Quarter Horses. The original mare we bought (Poco Roanoak) was ultimately to give me ten foals, counting the two already born and with her at the time of acquisition. Those two daughters, Poco Tami Bud, and Pocobud were to provide more. I purchased only one other mare during those breeding years who gave me three foals. The rest of the herd was from those foundation mares. We purchased a breeding stallion to save stud fees, boarding costs, and time and expense involved in hauling mares (who often had babies with them) to a stallion.

Pink Rey was 11 years old when we acquired him. He was a well-bred, good natured, beautiful stallion, who had been shown minimally in halter and pleasure as a very young horse and then went to the breeding shed where he was used exclusively for stud purposes until we purchased him. From the time we got him until his death, he was to be the sire of numerous good horses for us and many others as well.

We liked this stallion so much and saw definite potential in him to do more than propagate the species so we decided not to just breed him but to ride him and see if we could get more use out of him. With very little training he went on to become an excellent calf roping and barrel racing horse, even winning championships as a barrel horse for Laura Lee.

Having those mares and our own stallion led to many babies. I had so wanted them that each became like part of the family and I couldn't part with any. They were all special. At one point I had a herd of 35 and couldn't do much with many of them due to time restraints. Laura Lee was doing many of the chores, and riding many of the horses for me. I had a neighbor girl, Rachel, doing some chores as well as many other things for me. Even so, that many horses demanded more time and expense than we could afford. I was forced to cut down. Selling the first one was quite painful but it didn't take me long to realize that even one less was less expense and work. The second sale was a little easier. I got on a roll downsizing.

I donated many to Miracle Mountain Ranch, the Christian youth ranch with a horse program I'd sort of become a part of, and so it wasn't long before I was down to about a dozen or so. I liked it that way. As of this writing I am down to two and one of them is a broodmare, but more about that later. One of those we had until recently was Titan, the

27-year-old son of Pocobud. The average life expectancy of a horse is early to mid-twenties, yet he is still running barrels and chasing steers and shows no sign of slowing down. In fact, teamed up with Bill, and riding Titan, we won the team roping at our rodeo a few months ago.

We had some roping calves we brought to the farm with us and raised them up to begin building a herd for ourselves. They had the run of that big barn in the beginning. Now, to house the growing number of horses, we began crowding the cattle out of the barn little by little by building stalls for the horses beginning on the road end.

After winning a barrel racing futurity on Shane Bar Reed (the most talented offspring out of Poco Roanoak) and getting a sizable check for doing so, we used the winnings to build a pole barn to house mares and foals. It remained their domain until such time as I reduced the herd sufficiently to no longer need that barn for horses and it became our roping cattle barn.

A gravel pit we had purchased in 1975 had a large building on it that the previous owner had used as a sawmill. We converted a small shed attached to it into an office for the business and used the mill part as an indoor riding arena. We only knew of one or two other indoor arenas in the entire area and had long dreamed of having one of our own but never expected it to actually happen. We were so grateful for it in spite of the fact that it was not at our home and was extremely cold inside in the winter.

Every opportunity we had (that was winter due to working all hours the rest of the year) we loaded horses and traveled the 10 miles one way to use it. Randy and Scott and their friends used it even more than Bill, Laura Lee, and I did as they would spend weekends down there and play in it day and night. They rode, roped calves, and rode rough stock. They even built a bunk house of sorts for their overnight stays.

We would never have considered giving up this wonderful opportunity of riding indoors but after making that trip for several years and most often fighting ice and snow to get back up the hill to the farm, we were quite interested in the offer that came from an individual who wanted to purchase the arena to use for his show horses. He wanted the building and 10 acres of the over 110 acres we had with the gravel pit.

While we didn't want to give up the indoor arena it didn't take me long to figure out that with the money we would receive from the sale, we could build an arena at the farm. It sounded more and more like a good deal to us and thus we sold the property to him and did in turn put an indoor arena up at home. We had no more need to haul to use an indoor and now we also had our horses housed right where we would ride. The arena we put up at home was 20 feet wider and 16 feet longer than the one we sold and provided more room and opportunities, including the many competitions that would eventually be held in it.

As soon as the main part of the arena was built, we added 24 feet to one side and built 16 stalls down the entire length. A few years later we extended the roof beyond the stalls the entire length allowing for two very large pens which provide free access to pasture and protection for horses to live in.

Approximately 10 years after building the stalls we added room to the other side of the main arena and built two large "holding" areas where competitors and their horses can wait inside for their turn to compete in the arena, and a large clubhouse with a kitchen and two restrooms, complete with showers. A wash rack for the horses was built in one of the areas providing a place, at last, to hose down and bathe horses in this uncooperative climate.

With four gas wells drilled on the property and the ability to purchase gas at wellhead prices, we put up heaters and heated the indoor arena. (As of this writing, we now own the wells.) To someone who hates the cold, the value of that convenience is immeasurable. Many dreams came true for me with this project.

The arena at the gravel pit had doubled as our maintenance garage for the business equipment. Now that the property was sold we had no choice but to run the business from our home. The equipment was kept at the farm for the next several years. A large maintenance garage was built about 350 feet from the house for working on equipment, and a parking lot built next to it to keep our growing inventory of heavy equipment. The parking lot took up all the area surrounding the garage but was not adequate.

The men parked equipment and cars next to as well as on the yards and every available spot in the area. Disabled equipment waiting to be fixed, old things that never were to be fixed; all were kept here. It was quite the sight; heavy equipment and dump trucks parked all over the place.

The place looked like a construction site, used car lot, and junk yard rolled into one. It was my front yard. It was not a pretty sight and bothered me terribly.

Bill was extremely busy with work and had a mindset that working on a job was his only responsibility. He had little time away from work and while he did many large projects on the ranch along with occasionally helping with others, I spent 30 years patching old fences, tearing down older fences, putting up new fences with stakes and electric wire, and even getting to the point of installing Hi-T fence alone (after the posts were put in with the tractor and post pounder). I really didn't mind as long as I was able to get the work done without his help. I really love the work. At times friends and family (our son-in-law, Bruce put Hi-T fence around the entire perimeter of the farm) would be available for the big jobs and I was more than grateful for the help. I learned how to do a lot of things on my own simply out of sheer determination to get them done. When it was available I would use the back hoe to pull old posts and cart them away, but often I carried them all by hand. A four-wheeler was a distant dream at that time or perhaps not even a dream yet.

Lots of open space around the house invited flower gardens and Bill, with his experience in landscaping, was very good at building them. They were beautiful, admired by all, and so appreciated, but I was soon to find out that building them was as far as his interest in them went. They were left to me to maintain. This made more work for me and was not as enjoyable to me as tearing down and rebuilding.

Building wasn't just for structures though. With the arena and the competitions, a new area of building was beginning.

Chapter Twenty-Three

THE DRY PERIOD

Matthew 22:37: "Thou shalt love the Lord they God with all your heart, and all your soul and all your mind." (NKJV)

Rodeo had always been the most important activity away from work for Bill. Jumping had been my biggest love but with all leisure time spent at rodeos jumping was no longer an option for me and so I turned my attention to barrel racing. It was the only event open for women at that time. I loved it as well; the speed, the tight turns, and the excitement of competing in such an exciting environment. All three of our children were now involved in rodeo and all of us had close friends from outside areas we would only see at rodeos. It was the favorite part of our lives.

Then came a period of time when with one thing and another, we were not getting to many, if any, rodeos. This state of affairs continued for five years. We were busy building our new location, preparing for our new home, trying to hang onto the business, and many other things we could have attributed it to, and did at the time, but we were to realize later it was God's way of getting us out of an environment in which we were hesitant to take a stand for Him as we should. We were embarrassed to let our friends know how we felt about our Lord. How ashamed I am for that now. I believe God set us aside and used those five years to help us mature in our relationship with Him at least to the point where we weren't as reluctant to let people know where we stood.

As the end of that long stretch approached, we were at a rodeo in Attica, NY. While there a friend, Gary, was asking us yet another time to let him take us to this place called Circle C Ranch. He had asked many times before but we never had time to go and really weren't too interested in doing so.

Circle C is a Christian youth camp and they put on this little rodeo Saturday mornings during the camping season. This particular year we finished our competition at Attica on Friday night and weren't "up" (scheduled to compete) at Gerry, NY until Sunday afternoon. Gary pleaded with us to go with him to Circle C. It was practically on the way from one rodeo to the other. With all excuses gone we finally, reluctantly, agreed. It was August 1981.

We pulled into the ranch and looked for the rodeo arena. The most we found was a little area fenced off with some barbed wire. We were told there would be calf roping and went to find and check out the calves. It is a practice of ropers to check out the stock upon arrival to see the size, breed, and condition of the animals to determine ahead of time just how easy or difficult they may be to get to the ground and tie. What we found was one Holstein calf, not generally the preferred breed used in rodeo as they are most often too slow and also are not one of the strongest of calves.

When entering a rodeo we were familiar with the term "one head", but it meant you only got to chase one calf in one performance whereas some rodeos would give you two runs, one in each of two different performances. This then would be called a two-head rodeo. This "one-calf" rodeo gave new meaning to the term.

The "rodeo" at Circle C was mostly a time when the parents got to see their camper children perform simple games on horseback using slow, safe camp horses, a far cry from what we knew as rodeo. Despite these stark differences there was something about this place; something enticing that drew us back. We decided we would try it again.

From that first Saturday visit we made the trip back to Circle C Ranch every Saturday camp was open (with the exception of one), and many more days besides, for the next 20 years.

Not too long after we started making those trips to Circle C, our horse trailer broke down while at the ranch leaving us with no way to get our horses home. Chuck and Sonya Swain, new friends we met that very day at Circle C spoke right up and told us they would haul our horses the 115 miles home. We were astonished! They didn't even know us, yet they were willing to spend that much time just to help us out. We were also very grateful. Time only increased our love for one another and they became some of our dearest friends.

Another family we were blessed to get to know was the Choate's. A more fun loving family I've never met. Mom, Judy, was especially a blessing to everyone around her. Never without a smile, she was also never without encouragement. Her sons had a new love for rodeo, one specializing in bull riding, another in bronc riding; the third, a little smarter than the other two, abstained from both.

With our rodeo experience and their newfound love, their dad, Hugh, started buying and raising bucking bulls that were then used for the rodeos at Circle C. They used their well-bred AQHA mares for bucking horses, two of them going on to be used in professional rodeos. With the exuberance of the Choate's for rough stock and our love for roping and barrel racing, we made quite the production team.

Each Saturday we would load up calves, steers, horses, and as many people as we could round up and travel to the ranch to meet the Choate's with their broncs and bulls and put on a full-fledged rodeo, complete with specialty acts, for the campers and families. Each Saturday afternoon (or often Sunday afternoon) we would head back home. In time, we spent entire weeks at the ranch helping with family camps and other horse related events.

The time spent at this special place was to have a profound effect on our spiritual lives. As we were surrounded by Christians each weekend, we were learning from them how to live this Christian life we were committed to. In addition, we had the privilege of listening to Wes Aarum speak and preach on a regular basis. What a great time we had learning about our Lord in such an environment.

Wes is a past president of Youth for Christ in Canada and spent some time as the music director for Leighton Ford (Billy Graham's brother-in-law) crusades. He is the founder (and past President) of Living Waters Ministries (parent of Circle C) and has been involved in many other camp related missions. A.W. Tozer, a renowned author and preacher, was like a father to Wes and from him and other noted spiritual giants, he gleaned, devoured, and retained much of their teaching. An evangelist, Wes has traveled extensively preaching. Each time we heard him speak, we would be spellbound by his teachings. We couldn't help but be affected by the things he had to say and slowly but surely our lives began to reflect it.

Chapter Twenty-Four

THE "REAL" RODEO

Colossians 3:23: "And whatever you do, do it heartily, as to the Lord, and not to men." (NKJV)

The training period without the rodeos, the associated relationships with Circle C Ranch, and other spiritual growth factors, had made a profound effect on our lives. By the time God let us return to the rodeo arena He had shown us more of what He expected of us and how to accomplish what He asked. He gave us the courage and strength to show a difference in our lives when around nonChristians. Due to our commitment to Him and our desire to serve Him first, He also allowed us to begin a new venture.

Bill and I were youth leaders for the teenagers in our church in 1984. Most of the class was comprised of teenage boys and the girls, and those that attended, for the most part, were the adventurous type. During meetings we discussed personal things God was doing in our lives and of course, rodeo was mentioned often. The kids were very interested in the rodeo activities and since most of them had never seen one, they asked us to put a rodeo on for them. We decided it would be a fun thing to do and plans were made. With our children already professionals in their events we had all the contestants we needed right at home.

Our first rodeo was to be solely for our youth group and we were just going to do a few of the events. Before the date arrived, the word got out that we were having a rodeo and requests to attend began pouring in. By the time rodeo day came, much of the church family showed up along with some outside our church. Spectators sat on the ground, in lawn chairs, and on hay wagons. The announcer's stand was also a hay wagon and the sound system quite primitive.

This first rodeo was a huge success and was the beginning of the annual rodeo that has now been going strong every year to the final writing of this book. An evangelistic outreach of our church, it has had the full support of each and every pastor our church has had throughout most of those years. It is a professional rodeo in every sense of the word, providing bleacher seating for over 1500 spectators, and now an announcer's stand as well as proper sound equipment, and all else that is needed to make a first-class rodeo. With the exception of 2016, there has never been a charge for spectators to come and enjoy the action.

God has given us some help with friends that produce rodeos of their own and have been heavily involved in rodeo most of their lives. Over the past many years we have united with Cross Over The Line Rodeo Co. and have far surpassed my dreams for putting on a first-class professional rodeo. Fred, Michelle, and Louis Backlas – owners of the rodeo company – are such a blessing to us and the rodeo. They completely handle the rough stock end of things and help in many other ways from office work to announcing to gospel presentation.

With our rodeo friends and contacts, we have more than enough competitors that come to perform at their own expense. We have added events to excite the spectators and contestants alike and a good time is had by all.

Having a rodeo at our ranch has been an exciting venture, but God has used this rodeo to teach me further that things are to be done for Him, not for me. The purpose of the rodeo is not just to provide good clean family fun, but the message of God's love and gift of salvation through His Son, Jesus, is given for all to hear at each one. That is the real purpose.

I had a hard time getting it through my head that this rodeo is for the Lord, not me. Even though the rodeo is not until the third week in August, early in the spring of each year I began suffering anxiety as the enormous project of producing this rodeo lay before me. What if it rained and no one came? What if it was too slow? What if someone got hurt? What if I messed up the paperwork? The contestants are volunteers – what if not enough of them came? What will people think of the entire thing and of me as producer? The list of questions was endless, and Satan was to torture me with it for years.

It took many, many years before I came to the realization that this is not my rodeo, but God's, and that He is in charge of all those things I worried about. Each year I gave more of it up to His direction and finally, I went yet another step in giving it up to Him, asking Him to get me out of the way. I wanted no recognition for myself, but only to draw others to Him. The rodeo that followed this commitment was a good one. It rained all day on the rodeo, yet it was one of the best we've had and I was at peace throughout the entire thing – wet, but at peace.

Since that time the rodeos have been pretty much perfect in every way from weather to spectator response and everything in between. Praise God for His goodness and may He continue to reap a harvest from this unusual outreach. There is no way this side of heaven to imagine what God has accomplished through this opportunity.

Chapter Twenty-Five

THE TAMING OF THE SHREW

1 Peter 3:4: "Rather, it should be that of your inner self, the unfading beauty of a gentle and quiet spirit, which is of great worth in God's sight." (NIV)

In a Sunday school class many years ago the teacher was talking about the Bible passage in 1 Peter 3: 3, & 4, wherein it describes women with whom the Lord is obviously pleased. ("Your beauty should not come from outward adornment… Instead, it should be that of your inner self, the unfading beauty of a gentle and quiet spirit, which is of great worth in God's sight." (NIV) As the teacher read the passage, my husband, not one prone to *any* physical demonstration in public, elbowed me in the ribs – hard! I was infuriated and embarrassed as the entire class saw it. By his actions Bill was letting everyone there know just how far from this teaching my disposition was. While most of them didn't know me well enough to realize the truth of his insinuation, I felt irredeemable and unfixable as I knew he was right and I knew I would never attain that high and lofty goal set by the scriptures. Now all these years later I felt this was where the Lord was trying to lead me. Talk about an impossible task – it was not a comfortable time.

I was raised in an environment of sarcasm. Even what others referred to as kidding, and to them probably was, was done with sarcasm. In an effort to avoid it I drove myself to be perfect. If I did nothing to provoke them, perhaps they would just ignore my presence and not speak at all. It was no wonder as I grew up I also used sarcasm in most of my conversations, especially with family. God made me aware of this even if I said the right things, but had a sarcastic attitude. The things I said were of little value and worse yet a detriment to my profession of being a Christian. It took many painful years for me to allow Him to re-construct my ways of thinking and more to change my ways of reacting to and acting in adverse situations – even more to change the tone of my voice.

For the most part I was never happy in my marriage. I felt terribly unloved and out of place most of the time. I longed for things to help me forget the many hurts I had, even for a little space in time. During the early years, in addition to my time spent riding and working with the horses and dogs, I began reading romance novels. I devoured story after story and as I did, I got less and less satisfied with, and more and more miserable in my marriage. I knew these types of books weren't helping me with my attitude and longings, but I knew of nothing better to read – and I loved to read. I enjoyed the momentary escape they provided. I was also wrapped up in soap operas, further increasing my dissatisfaction with my unromantic life. My music tastes were the country songs that portrayed loneliness and illicit affairs. As the years rolled by and my faith and trust in the Lord for my circumstances increased, I felt guilty about the things I was reading and listening to and the longings the books and music gave me for a different life. I needed something else.

The search was on and I discovered, much to my surprise, there were Christian books and music to be found but even as I discovered their availability I was sure they would be dull and boring. In an effort to do right I chose a couple of books and decided to give them a try. Amazed at the interesting content of them I began to read as many of them as I could.

I read books that told interesting stories of other's lives and then I started reading "how to" books; how to be a happy wife, how to be the wife of a happy husband, Spirit controlled temperaments, etc. While I felt their writings were far beyond what I would ever attain, they were of help to me and led me on a path of better understanding of relationship issues and a desire to work to make my own relationship better. Listening to mostly or only Christian music developed much later as I found it difficult to enjoy the style of the Christian music available at the time. My taste is definitely "country".

I had so many issues with Bill and his ways of dealing with things that it was having severe, adverse effects on me. I had become bitter, resentful, angry, and most of the time quite sarcastic. I was miserable and my family was well aware of it. I hated situations and conditions I found myself in and hated that I was powerless to do anything to change them. That is a difficult place to get out of and I knew it would take a lot of giving up and giving in on my part. That went against my very nature and everything I felt at the time. Part of me knew I needed to change but most of me said none of it was my fault and I shouldn't have to. I tried to change, at times, to be what I thought he wanted me to be. It did not work. Neither one of us liked me. I did not know where to begin to get it right. I needed something to be different though to get me off this path of self-destruction.

In desperation I got to the point where I would get up in the night and go to the living room, kneel down at the couch and cry out to God for relief. I would say, "Lord, you have to do something about Bill. I can't take anymore." Each time I did so, I would feel the definite question coming back from Him, "What about you, Joan?" to which I responded with, "But, Lord, You see what he is doing. You know he is wrong. Something needs to be done about him and the situation." Each time I did so, I received the same response. "What about you, Joan?" It always came back to me. I was frustrated and I felt betrayed by my God. Just as before it seemed He only cared about the other party. Didn't he care about me and my needs? Why would He defend Bill and tell me I had to be the one to change?

All my life I had a problem with fairness. I couldn't abide things being unfair and always did whatever I could to see that situations were dealt with fairly. I believe I caused problems with my children as I was always jumping into the middle of their arguments to try to make sure they were resolved fairly. I think it would have been better had I let them work more things out on their own. When I was powerless to make all things fair, it was almost more than I could bear. Now God was telling me to ignore things obviously terribly unfair and worse than that, to change the way *I* was thinking and speaking about things regardless of whether or not the other party changed. It was too much!

In time I realized it was my personal relationship with God that was the primary, and most important issue – not my relationship with Bill – that was at stake; further it was *my* responsibility to change, but I was not capable of handling this latest mandate from God. Even so I knew I had to find a way to try. Deep down I knew God's way was the only way even if I didn't like it. Knowing that and doing something about it though were two different things. I wasn't willing for God to make those changes in my life. It wasn't fair!

While searching for a solution, a statement Lillian Fuessler (the teacher who had taught that lesson on the meek and gentle spirit so long ago) had made came to the forefront of my mind and after struggling for a long time I got to the point where I was able to make that statement to God: "Lord, I am willing to be made willing". I even did that with hesitation and fear.

Bill and I had many difficulties. His controlling always-right character and my quick-to-answer-and-set-things-straight, and usually sarcastic mouth, clashed horribly. We worked together and had to work out every situation whether business, personal, family, or farm. We agreed on nothing and both tried to be the boss. He would not discuss any situation and he would not listen to anything I said – it was his way only, and if I even tried to present an idea, he would get extremely angry and tell me to quit arguing all the time. Other than that he basically did not communicate at all. I did drop many issues that should have been talked out because if I said anymore about it he would get angry and do nothing for me for days or even weeks.

I was afraid of what would happen to the business and us personally when he got into these moods, so I gave in. He blamed me for every adverse situation in the business finances and anywhere anything went wrong. One small example is the time he wanted a check for something and even after I told him there was no money, he said "Give me the check and you just see that some money is there". He took the check. I told him I had no place to get any money, but it fell on deaf ears. He spent the check, it bounced, and he blamed me for giving him a check that was worthless. This type of thing happened frequently in several areas. So many times I wanted to give up, to pack up, and move away. At times it seemed suicide would be the only way out. I had no answers, and I couldn't continue to live as we were.

Often I made plans to leave – at one point on the advice of a highly respected male Christian counselor – even for a short time but I was never able to go through with them. I didn't know where to go and I really didn't want everyone to know I couldn't handle things – that even with God I couldn't make it work. Making it more difficult to leave was the fact that I didn't want our children to know just how bad things were between their father and me. I didn't want to uproot them and draw them further into our problems.

I didn't want to leave my animals and couldn't take them all with me. Everything I wanted was on the farm and I felt if unfair that I should give it up because of him. In addition to that I had a deep sense of responsibility for the business and couldn't leave Bill to flounder alone. I knew he wouldn't make it without me and I would be to blame for his failure.

I was aware of the constant state of anger I was in. I excused it all as I had a lot of good reasons for being angry. Bill was my main reason. In addition to the things mentioned elsewhere, he was never there, we never talked, he knew of the problems with his family and did nothing about it; the list went on. The way I acted was his fault, no doubt. I believed that for many years and learned that actually there was some truth to it. If he had been the kind of husband God would have him be, if he had put me first, had cherished me, had cared for me, I may have been quite different. It didn't happen that way, though, and I was angry about it. I felt very unimportant in his life. Maybe I was; maybe he had too many problems of his own to be too concerned about mine. I'm sure he didn't know what to do about most of them or how to deal with me anyway.

The story was told, by his mother, how she responded when he was little and he was accused of any wrong doing. The response was with the words that became classic in any conversation relating to such matters: "Not my Billy". We teased her about it in later years and still tease about it to this day. Part of the reason he seemed so self-centered was likely due to the fact that in his mother's eyes he could do no wrong, so if wrong was done between the two of us, it certainly had to be me doing it. Even in the situations where problems occurred with his siblings, ultimately the blame was cast on me. Not from Bill in those cases (he knew the truth and was on my side) but from his mother. I drove him to it; it was my idea, etc. It couldn't have been her Billy.

There was a Mother's Day when Bill did not feel like driving the 23 miles to his mother's house to see her. I had taken Laura Lee and one of our horses to a horse show in the morning to let her show and to spend some time with her. I told Bill he should take the boys and go see his mother while we were gone. We came home and found him and the boys in the basement playing ping pong. I asked him if he went to see his mother. He said he didn't feel like it. I repeatedly told him if he was not going to go see her, he'd better at least call her. He didn't do that either.

A short time later, the phone rang. I answered it and took a terrible tongue lashing from my mother-in-law about not letting her son come in to see her! Of course I didn't tell her he didn't want to; I didn't say anything. Bill never responded one way or the other. She also, yelling at me yet, told me she was coming out and demanding the truth about the business break-up. I told her she would have to talk to Bill about that. She said she definitely would. She didn't come out that day and never brought it up again.

Due to the blood clot complications after our daughter was born my doctor told me I must not ever be pregnant again. He bluntly told me should that happen, "You will be dead before you even know you're pregnant". Surgery was almost as big a risk for me as the pregnancy would have been so I begged Bill to take my place and have the surgery necessary to protect me. He was fearful and would not consider having anything done to him leaving me no choice but to take the huge risk involved. His mother was concerned about his pleasures until I would be recovered enough from the blood clot surgery to undergo the sterilization surgery. Her unmasked concern for her son and total lack of concern for me did nothing to improve our relationship. Understandably, I suppose she was still suffering with what I had done to ruin her son's life as it must have appeared to her. Between the two of them, I felt like a worthless, replaceable object, unworthy of consideration.

As part of the "taming" process, God had to deal with my perpetual state of anger. As I write, I remember times of anger, and the manifestations of that anger. To arouse that anger didn't take anything more than *my* needs weren't being met. I had many thoughts of "I deserved this or I should or should not be treated like that. I should be thought of once in a while."

One incident of extreme anger that remains strong in my memory is that of me being in the back yard on top of the station wagon, waxing the roof, while Bill pursued his favorite past time being in the arena roping calves. That I wasn't helping him tells me I was very angry. I always saddled his horses, warmed them up for him until they were ready for him to step up on and use, cooled them out for him, cleaned them up and put them away. I did this at home and I did it when we were on the road.

This particular day he was using a horse that was not the most solid and reliable, chasing a Brahman calf we had at the time that was big, fast, and feisty. Unfortunately for him, he caught it. He jumped off the horse and ran for the calf but the horse didn't stop as well as he should have and left slack in the rope. Bill turned to make the horse work the rope and the calf made a turn in the arena heading back for Bill.

With the slack rope, the calf went between Bill and the horse and when the maneuvering was done the rope was in a half-hitch around Bill's body with the horse, now working as he should and pulling the rope tight, backing one direction and the calf trying to get away by running the other. He was in a potentially dangerous situation I knew. As I watched I thought to myself: "I hope you get killed". I was angry enough that I meant it. There were many times I thought about how I would like to see him dead.

I recall an evening when we were fighting and I stormed out of the house, walked across the field to my mother's back yard, and strolled on down the slope to the creek. I felt completely hopeless as I could not get through to my husband and I hated my life the way it was. As I walked there by the creek it was just beyond twilight making it difficult to see things clearly. I was engrossed in my self-pity, not paying attention to things around me and I came upon a skunk. I nearly stepped on it! I scared it every bit as much as it scared me and it let me have it, both barrels, as the saying goes. What a shock!

I immediately headed home and proceeded to march into the house through the back door. Bill smelled me and immediately put me back out the door ordering me to strip there and leave my clothes outside. I obeyed, but still angry, stomped up the stairs and threw myself into bed. Mistake! Now the bedding was tainted. I took it and threw it outside with my clothes and took a shower – didn't help. What a mess! Before the ordeal was over, I had bathed and washed my hair in tomato juice and buried my clothes and bedding in a pile of dirt for several days before laundering and finally being rid of the smell.

Years later when I thought most of this anger was under control I had yet another incident of "Your punishment will be swift and sure" when I was feeding horses one morning. I had a mare in the indoor arena next to the stalls raising quite the fuss while I fed the other horses already in their stalls. She was rearing at the gate and acting quite unruly. I don't deal well with that.

I was carrying feed in a small rubber bucket, which was now empty in my hand. I turned it upside down and banged it on the gate right by her nose in an attempt to scare her enough to get away from the gate and be patient until I came for her. I hit the gate with enough force that the bucket sprang back and whacked me right in the face, the nose to be exact, and broke my nose, this being about the sixth time it was broken. I was furious and angrier than ever.

There were the many times when in anger I would try to slap a misbehaving horse with a lead rope only to cause me some real pain when the snap came back and landed somewhere on my body, often my head or hand. It never hurt the horse. Again, I would be angrier than when I started out.

I had never had any self-esteem or self-worth. I felt like such a failure, especially as a wife. I often played scenarios in my mind in which I would die and God would give (I even knew who she was, "she" being different women over the years that I thought would be better for him) some other woman to him that would be much better than me and make him happy as I couldn't. With all the sarcasm from my family, the problems with Bill and his family, the anger and resentment I harbored, the mistakes and messes I'd made with my mouth, I felt helpless and hopeless to ever see things be different for me.

Even as a Christian, I still thought of suicide often. It seemed the only way out. How simple it would be. While driving I would see a tractor trailer heading rapidly my way and think of how quick and easy it would be to drive into his lane at the last moment and just get out of this entire mess. Caring for others the way I did, I could not bring myself to do such a thing to the unsuspecting and innocent driver that would feel responsible for my death. Much thought was also given to the accident only crippling me. That was a deterrent.

I thought how quickly and easily I could shoot myself but that took more planning and time, not a spontaneous move as the vehicular scenario was. If I took the time to plan it, I invariably found too many reasons not to do it. Sometimes it made me angry to think that I had to go to that extent to make Bill see what he was doing to me and to take me seriously when I told him I couldn't handle life the way it was. I knew it would shock him should I go through with it and he would regret he didn't do something about it when he could have, but it would then be too late.

Most often it was our children that gave me the incentive to go on. I loved them and did not want to put them through such an ordeal. There was also the age old question, "Would I go to heaven if I committed this sin?" Where could I turn?

One day, on the drive home from the office in Waterford, I was having the same negative thoughts running rampant through my mind: "You can't change. You'll never see him change. You are so far from what God wants you to be, you'll never get there. Things are such a mess they won't ever be any better," and so on. I was thinking of suicide yet again as the final answer to some rest from all the problems and hassles. As these thoughts were having their way with my mind, a new thought occurred to me, seemingly out of nowhere. (I knew it came from the Lord.) It said simply: "God loves you. He loves you just the way you are and where you are in life at the moment." I was astounded and spent some time thinking about that. I then made a very wise and important choice. I chose to believe it.

Choosing to believe it I thought about that statement; and as I dwelled on it for a time, it made me focus on the magnitude of God. God; the God who spoke creation into being, the God who created life, nature, and all the intricacies of each, the God who did miracles from time immemorial and still does today; this God says He loves *me*! Well, I reasoned, if God says He loves me and I believe God to not just tell the truth, but to *be* Truth, then I must actually have some worth! This revelation was to provide two things for me – most importantly, the realization that I did not have to be perfect.

I always tried to be perfect. I wouldn't let anyone help me with anything. I had to do it all even though I had more to do than was humanly possible. I felt it would be weak and diminish my self-esteem if I asked for help. I needed recognition for something and if working hard was all I had, so be it, but it was so taxing emotionally to fall continually so short of the mark. Now God was showing me it was okay if I wasn't perfect because He would forgive me for my imperfections. I was learning He loved me enough to help me become more of what He wanted me to be. It also gave me a big sense of freedom to stop worrying quite so much about myself – to look beyond myself, and to begin to see others around me that needed love and understanding.

As I tried to be more Christ-like in behavior, I read a lot of material on making my marriage work, developing a better personality, and such subjects. I began putting some of this advice into practice. Nothing was easy in the beginning. I would make a vow to myself that I wouldn't react in a certain way or would act another way and fail repeatedly to follow through correctly. I would then feel defeated and want to quit. But God would pick me up and set me on my feet to go try again.

Even as I learned to say the right things in response to situations, most often that response was still given with sarcasm. Even harder than forcing myself to give the right response was learning not to respond at all. I was never one to let something go when it was wrong and I never planned on doing so. There were women I'd heard of who say the success of their marriage was attributed to keeping their mouths shut where their husbands were concerned. I considered them fools and felt they didn't know how to do things right. Giving in was not an option for me. I didn't want to change that much, but God knew I needed to. As I struggled along and let Him have more control of my life, ever so slowly I began to see some change.

Our children were now all married and out of the house and my struggle with God and my disposition was continuing. A turning point came on a Sunday evening when Bill and I were having yet another argument (seemed it always happened around the time we headed to church). This time God suddenly and clearly made me see for the first time that our bickering was not only harmful to our relationship, and the witness we were to those who were subjected to our behavior, but that we were bringing sorrow to Him! We, the Christians, the ones who proclaim love for him, the leaders of various groups and projects in our church, were letting Satan have numerous victories over us by falling into this cleverly set trap of his. We were breaking God's heart each and every time we gave in to our selfish thoughts and actions. I became angry about the failure the situation caused and vowed to make a change. Slowly it became easier to turn to Him each time I felt the need to answer and argue and at least try to hear Him and do it His way.

Thinking more about the Lord and what my sin was doing to Him made me search even deeper for the true reason behind my praying. In every instance it was something good I wanted from God and for a lot of the right reasons. But as God was able to get through to me, He was able to show me the true motive behind almost every request and I didn't like what He was showing me. His Holy Spirit gently pointed out to me that what I really wanted was for things to go better for family, work, and others as that would ultimately make things a lot better for me.

Behind my prayers was a deep seated and well-disguised selfishness. I didn't want my life upset. I didn't want the worries that broken relationships might cause in the family and the business. This revelation ultimately made me realize I did not trust God nearly as much as I had thought. Once I got that realization out in the open it helped me give more control to Him and forced me to stop trying to manipulate God into doing things my way. It took many more years before I truly discovered He only wants what's best for me anyway!

In an effort to make things better I began to involve God more in my problems and situations. When Bill would be unfair, too harsh, too rigid, too unforgiving, instead of starting a ruckus over it I would go to God and call out to Him for His intervention in the matter. It was obvious that if Bill was different in many areas things would be much better for many people in the home and the work place. Very often I didn't see the results I was looking for and I was disappointed in God's methods and timing. I had a very difficult time understanding the entire process of praying for things to be better.

As I struggled with this and as I grew in my knowledge and relationship with the Lord, I was able to listen more and ask less. Oh, the same needs were there but I was beginning to listen to Him instead of continually telling Him what I *thought* needed changed and began letting Him make the changes He *knew* needed to be made.

I won't take the time or space to tell all the steps, (although I have noticed this is the longest chapter in this book) but I learned that a truly Biblically submissive wife is a happier woman, that God is the One who will do the changing of my husband in His way and His time; that it is my responsibility to let Him make me what He wants *me* to be, and leave the rest up to Him. When I did just that, He made remarkable changes in Bill that far exceeded my hopes and certainly my expectations. We began to enjoy each other in ways never before possible. I was reminded of God's word when He promises to "redeem the time…": He did that for Bill and me. Our latter years of marriage were good years – years without all that strife and discontentment. We learned how to truly love and care for one another. I was surprised and grateful for the way God made a few good years wipe out the emotional stigma 35 tension-filled ones had created.

I will also tell you, with God's help, I was able to put a lot of past hurts aside and begin to develop a better relationship with Bill's parents to the point that his father thought I was pretty special before he died (he thought I was the *best* country singer!) and his mother and I had developed a genuine love and affection for each other. We never talked about those early days; the need to exonerate myself vanished, and I never told her any of the negative things of others she loved – it didn't matter by that time. I was more interested in her happiness than my gratification. A special treat was leading her to a saving knowledge of Jesus Christ and knowing I'll see her again! She is gone to be with the Lord, now, and I miss her.

The author with her husband Bill, 1958

Bill and Joan, 1960

Bill and Joan

Joan and Bill, 2000

Pal

Pal

Midnight

Hunter's Lodge

Remodeled Chicken Coop

Home on Footmill Road

And Finally, Home Sweet Home!

Joan and Bill Team Roping

Chapter Twenty-Six

UNCONDITIONAL LOVE

1 Corinthians 13:4a: "Love suffers long and is kind." (NKJV)

Think about the term "unconditional love". What it means is "love with no conditions attached such as "I'll love you if." I was raised to understand that if you behaved you didn't get punished; if you did this, maybe I would do something for you. It was that simple. If you were out of line in the least bit, punishment would be swift and sure. I believe my mother loved me, but no one ever taught her to show it, so I had no understanding of it. My parents never told me they loved me as I grew up.

We are a product of our environment to a certain degree. We can only pass on what we know and have been taught. There is no crime in the things we don't know. The crime develops when we come to a point in our lives where we recognize there is a better way – the right way, but refuse to go to the trouble to change. We blame our parents, our circumstances, people, and say we can't help it. We say the damage has been done and that's the way we are. So we go on and cause the same insecurities in our children and children's children. That is a crime and that crime even has a name – selfishness. Now selfishness can cause all sorts of evils and problems, and, unfortunately, none of us have to be taught how to be selfish. It is born in us. Some of us develop it to a greater degree than others, true, but it's an easy thing to acquire.

Self*less*ness, on the other hand, is a far harder thing to come by. It means putting all our own desires behind us and looking only to the welfare of others. This is a very difficult task with no example or teaching. But while we are quick to blame our parents and past, we must always realize that we have the supreme example and teacher of unconditional love, Jesus Christ. He can enable us to do the impossible.

There are many things I'd like to accomplish in telling some of Scott's and my story. I would like people to understand some of Scott's struggles, to see the good side and the "bad" side of him, to identify with both, and to see similarities in their own relationships. Perhaps some will find help and comfort in our experiences. I don't think a mother can tell the story of her son without telling somewhat of her own at the same time. What I will attempt to convey to you is a glimpse of the lessons I learned from Scott – the things he had no idea he was teaching me.

He was a beautiful baby with lots of dark hair and big dark eyes. I was 18 years old, and he was my second child: I was a child myself. He was a happy child, always smiling. I, on the other hand, was happy and smiling on the outside but lonely, trapped, and anxious on the inside. He was an adventurous child always on the move. I was a homebody, never wanting to be anywhere else. He was a busy boy, always into something, always on the go. With two babies and being immature, I just wanted some peace and quiet and to be able to do something I wanted to do. He, like all children, needed an abundance of love. He got what I understood to be that love – good care, constant supervision, consistent discipline. I was to find out later that was not enough or the right way to do it, but I could only give what I understood love to be and I was not to find out until many years later what love really was. Scott was going to help me do that.

When I was 15, and nine and a half years after my younger sister was born, my mother had her last child; a son. He was a handsome child. My father had not wanted another child but my mother insisted – she usually got what she wanted. My mother adored him. He grew up normally, if not a bit spoiled, but as he entered his teenage years he began having some problems in school and was diagnosed as hyperactive. He was put on medication which helped some. What I thought I saw happening was that each infraction my brother made was excused by my mother assaying, "He's hyperactive". We older children got punished, and sometimes severely; Dan got spoken to, or excused, not punished in the way we were.

He began drinking and then driving and drinking. It got him into trouble and he ended up in jail more than once. Each time he was jailed, my parents bailed him out. After my mother died, my father continued the practice. Ultimately that brother was to spend 10 years of his life in prison for drinking related issues. He still has a severe drinking problem and suffers from the consequences of that destructive behavior in a major way today. He basically has no life apart from being totally intoxicated.

Our son, Scott, was like my brother in many ways. He, too, had problems in school. He, too, was diagnosed as hyperactive. He, too, was put on medication. The difference is that I didn't keep him on it. I'm not sure if that was a wise decision or not, but I had watched and seen the problems with my brother and I didn't accept that they were all medical. I thought he was spoiled. I was scared to death my son would end up like my brother.

When he was 17, Scott ran away from home for the first time. Upon finding out, I sat down at the dining room table. The fear and pain I was feeling was unbelievable and almost paralyzing. I'd never felt anything like it before. I moaned to the Lord. I said to Bill, "If God doesn't do something for me in 10 minutes, I'll absolutely die!" I meant it; I felt I really would.

I had just found the note in Scott's room. "Dear Mom: I had to leave. I'm sorry. I love you, Scott". I had no idea where he'd gone. I didn't know where to begin to find him. I just knew if I didn't, I was in serious emotional trouble. I didn't even attempt to track him down. In the first place, I couldn't. I was frozen to that chair, looking out over the back pasture to the woods, stark terror gripping my heart. Secondly, I instinctively knew I wasn't going to find him if I tried. I needed the Lord to do it for me. About 10 minutes later the phone rang. It was Scott calling from Fort Worth, TX. He had flown out there with a friend. Already not liking it and feeling homesick, he made arrangements to come back and was home that evening. I rejoiced in the Lord's goodness.

It was only the beginning. Scott couldn't stay home for any length of time. He was not permitted to smoke or drink in our home and he wanted to do both. He had friends who lived in whatever manner they chose in their home so he would stay with them. They could have girlfriends there, drink or take whatever drugs they wanted, and live totally uninhibited. It was quite enticing for a teenager and very difficult for me to compete with.

I had nowhere to turn – no human to turn to, with the exception of a conversation with one of his teachers who was also a Christian counselor. I didn't think that was going in the right direction or going to be very helpful as one of the first things he asked me about was my relationship with my mother. I told him that had nothing to do with the situation and he proceeded to explain to me why it had everything to do with it. I listened and went to work on it. (It did open my eyes to the reality of the importance of our relationship with our parents, and God did a wonderful healing in that area as well.) I turned to God. I begged Him to spare my son. I begged for wisdom and most of all, I begged for unconditional love for my son. I didn't feel like loving him. I wanted to tell him off and to let him know what his antics were doing to us. I certainly had no idea what unconditional love was as it was never demonstrated to me.

Fortunately, God knew the true desire of my heart was to salvage the relationship and to do it His way. He wanted to teach me to love the sinner while hating the sin. It was so hard! This concept of loving the child while hating the sin in his life helped me understand more of God's way of "thinking". That is exactly the way He sees us. He loves us no matter what, yet He cannot bear to look upon the sin in our lives. How remorseful I felt for all the anguish I caused Him. I prayed, I cried, I read God's promises. At times I was so angry with Scott I wanted to really let him have it verbally. In God's grace, He never let me find my son in those infuriating moments. Had I done so, I would have thrown the whole "unconditional love" idea away I'm sure.

With God's help and guidance, I was able to keep the lines of communication open. Scott would call on occasion and ask to be picked up and brought home. He would stay for a half a day, a whole day sometimes, but not long. He needed to get back to his habits. One Sunday he called and we picked him up at some girl's house he had spent the night with. He was dirty, unkempt, and showing all the signs of a bad hangover. He wanted to come home for a while. As the three of us rode toward home in the front seat of our pickup truck, I was prompted by God to say something to him. I remember clearly telling him (and I can remember the exact spot in our travels as well) "Scott, I want you to know that while I hate what you are doing, I love you. I love you no matter what you are doing as much as I love your brother who is home doing what we want him to do." The love I felt for him at that time was a genuine unconditional love. I believe he recognized that and I believe those words found soil in his heart in which to grow.

On one occasion I got a call from one of the Erie hospitals informing me Scott was in the emergency room and I should come in. When I arrived, a group of people from the family he was staying with was waiting outside his door as if he belonged to them. I felt so out of place and alone. The doctor came out of the room and seeing me standing there alone, asked if I was his mother. When I replied in the affirmative he took me alone into the room. How grateful I was for that act.

Scott was lying there, trembling from shock. He was already in a cast for a broken ankle suffered in a roller skating mishap. Now he had been too close to the fireplace in this other family's home when a waste basket from the bathroom was emptied into the fire (they were cold and had no other source of heat but to burn all they could find) resulting in an explosion from an aerosol can that had been in the basket. His face was burned along with a few other parts of his body. At least it was nothing life threatening. I will forever remember how his trembling subsided when I went in and laid my hand on his charred forehead. He was ordered to stay in the hospital for a few days. He left on his own later that day. He needed to get where he could drink and smoke.

It was January of 1979. Scott was 18 and his shenanigans had been going on for a year or more. After 19 years of marriage, Bill and I went away on our first vacation and we were two days into it, getting as far as northern Florida. Randy was going to drive down separately a week later with his brother and sister and join us but we were going to have some much needed time alone. Scott had actually come back and had been home for a couple of days and I thought things were turning around. I had been so looking forward to this time and it was already wonderful. We got to Florida, checked into a motel and called home to see how things were going, this being the first time we'd ever left them. A short time into the conversation we discovered Scott had already gone back to his friends. We were ready to pack up and head back home. I was in deep anguish over the situation. I could bear no more.

A short time before this I had read of someone who had gotten a hold of God in a very real way in a bad situation. I knew I needed a similar experience. I sat in the middle of the bed, cried to the Lord, and told Him I would not leave that spot until I had an answer and peace. I told Him I absolutely could take no more of all this worry about my son. I don't know how long it took, but He answered that prayer. After that period of calling on Him, I felt the peace and comfort I needed.

I felt the promise that God would save Scott and the assurance that he would not die until he was, indeed, saved and secure for eternity with God. God's assurance was so complete that I can honestly say I never again worried about Scott as I had done in the past. There were many trials ahead of me, but the worry was gone. I never doubted God on His word to me. No, things weren't different, but I was. I did not worry. I knew that whatever God allowed or brought into our lives would be in His control and He would allow it for our best. The vacation was restful and enjoyable and was needed for what was waiting ahead.

Scott was good natured, fun loving, and always had a heart for God. I have no doubt about that. He just had a hard time following Him closely with the worldly friends and pressures he had. He was up and down like a roller coaster in his Christian as well as his personal life. When he was down, he was really down and he generally got into trouble. He was not a leader, but more of a follower. This seemed to be the pattern of his life. During this particular time, and in just an 18-month period, Scott totaled three vehicles. These wrecks were not just fender benders yet in all cases he was able to walk away. I felt the hand of God on his life. I did not worry.

Things remained strained and hard for several years. Scott had a particularly hard time getting along with his father. I believe them being too much alike may have been a large part of it, but I believe Scott was suffering from the days when his father only worked or played for his own enjoyment, the multitude of broken promises he made to him, and the tension in the home. Bill barked orders, never showing much affection to the boys. Another factor in Scott's neediness may have been the fact that he and his brother spent a great deal of time with Bev's dad, Robert, until they were about five years old and then he seemed to just drop them. Scott wasn't dealing with that well and I feel rejection may have been a large part of what he struggled with.

In time he began to grow up, probably just stuffing his painful emotions deep inside, found the girl he loved as much as life itself and married her. They lived with us for a time, while here their first child was born; they then moved to the end of our property. His wife was like a daughter to me and I loved her dearly. She fit right in and became like a sister to our Laura Lee. We all had great times together. Scott and Michelle spent their spare time at the ranch, riding and roping. Bill was a header, Scott was his heeling partner. Bill worked with Scott on jobs and we saw him day and night, seven days a week. Bill and his son were becoming closer and I was happy to see it.

Scott and I talked a lot – many times late at night. I would awaken from sleep, often after midnight, to find him standing next to my bed saying "Mom, I need to talk". I would get up; we would go into the kitchen and talk. There were a lot of things he didn't understand about his relationship with his father and he didn't know how to deal with them. I wasn't as much help as I would have like to have been as I was struggling with some of the same things myself and didn't know what to do about them. He was hoping I could give him some answers: I was looking for some myself. I was able to give some help but I couldn't make everything okay the way I could when he hurt himself as a child. He was so needy and it broke my heart.

Scott had a big battle raging inside of him. He was trying and he was struggling. There were many dragons in his life and with the Lord's help he was slaying them, ever so slowly, one by one. One thing remained constant throughout the battles, whether won or lost. He wanted to be what God wanted him to be. He fell short of the mark more times than not, but he did have a heart for God.

God gave me an extraordinary and wonderful relationship with this remarkable child and I will be eternally grateful for it. I learned so much about love from him and learned to love him in a way I didn't know possible. I learned to put aside my hurts and desires and to look only for his needs.

Chapter Twenty-Seven

THE LAST PRAYER

Psalm 88:2b: "Let my prayer come before You; incline Your ear to my cry." (NKJV)

It was the middle of December, 1990: Scott was 29 years old. We had our company employee Christmas party that night at a local restaurant. After it was over, we returned home. A short time later Scott called from his home and asked if he could come up and talk. He arrived a few moments later. Usually Bill would leave and just the two of us would talk. This time he asked his father specifically to stay: He did.

We talked about several things, again mostly related to him and his father. I believe it was the only time the three of us addressed the issues hanging between the two men. It was a productive time and I believe even more understanding was gained between father and son. I rejoiced in the Lord. When talk dwindled down, I asked them if we could all pray together for the needs that had been expressed. They both readily agreed.

We sat in three separate chairs in a triangle formation facing one another. We took turns praying. However, when the last "Amen" was said, Scott spoke up again, saying, "Can I pray a little more? There's something specific I need to pray about." Of course, we agreed. At that time Scott did something very unusual for him; in fact, I'd never seen him do it before. He got up from his chair, turned around, and knelt in front of it. He then began to pray this way: "Thank you, Lord, for saving me. Thank you for all you do for my life. But Lord there is something I need to confess. You know, Lord, how jealous I have always been of my brother and the way I've felt about that. I'm so sorry for being selfish, Lord, as you know how much I love him. Lord, I want more than anything for my brother to be saved and be sure he is going to heaven. I am asking You to save him, no matter what it takes. I am willing to give up my life if it would mean he would get saved. In Jesus' name amen."

I was astounded as I listened to those words. It wasn't just the spoken words, but the brokenness and sincerity of the one speaking them. When Scott left for home, I said to Bill that I felt we had been in the presence of a spiritual giant. What a gift from God to help us face what the near future held.

Chapter Twenty-Eight

YEA, THOUGH I WALK

(The broken promise that could not be fixed)

Psalm 23:4 "Yea, though I walk through the valley of the shadow of death, I will fear no evil; for You are with me. (NKJV)

Scott had two children – his first, a son who was also our first grandchild. What a difference this child made in our lives! We were so busy and caught up with ourselves when our children were small and now we were oh, so much wiser. Michael was a beautiful, blue eyed blonde and a joy to be around.

After having little time and energy to spend with his own children, I was amazed at how Bill took to this grandchild. While Bill wasn't into changing diapers and that sort of thing, he was delighted to take Michael with him when he got a little older – even as a one-year-old. He would take him for an entire day and they spent many, many days together. They were inseparable. When Michael wasn't with Bill, he was likely to be here, playing by himself around the bucking chutes in the arena. He was a very happy child, and we were happy to have him.-

His sister, Jamie, was born when Michael was 15 months old. She was born in our house and was a beautiful child from the get-go. Jamie had to take a bit of a back seat as Michael was already traveling with his grandfather and old enough to not be as much work as a baby. For Bill to take care of one child by himself was quite a feat; there was no way he could handle two and Michael being older was easier and had already formed a strong bond with both Bill and I. I had no more time than I ever did. That made it difficult for Jamie to experience the same closeness with us and that would take its toll on her emotionally.

As she grew it became apparent that Jamie was horse crazy. While her brother was content to pretend he was bull riding and/or roping, Jamie wanted to ride and she wanted to barrel race.

I had a very good barrel horse while Jamie was in her early years. It was winning regularly for Laura Lee and me. When Jamie was six I told her mom I felt she was ready to ride Vivacious Jet (better known as Pally). She and almost everyone else thought I was nuts and was going to get her hurt. I knew the timing was right and was not worried about them together and her mother reluctantly agreed to let me try. I had let Jamie ride her just a time or two and she had done extremely well. She was so excited that she could ride this fabulous horse! Always wanting to please her father, she wanted him to witness this great accomplishment and asked him to come up to the barn one particular evening, a Saturday, to watch her ride. He promised he would but he wanted to eat dinner first. We already had the horse ready and left her saddled so we wouldn't hold him up when he did come.

Dinner was over and it was time to watch Jamie ride, but Scott didn't come to the barn. Instead Jamie and Michelle came back up and we unsaddled the mare. Scott's friends had shown up at his house and persuaded him to go four wheeling with them. Jamie was heartbroken. Scott then promised her he would definitely watch her ride Pally the next day after church and I tried to console her with telling her she would have more time to ride her the next afternoon and it would be just fine.

Scott never returned home that night and never saw his daughter ride this special horse. It will trouble Jamie to her death. Jamie went on to win many awards running barrels on Pally and he never saw any of them. He put this obligation off one time too many.

Horses have remained very important to Jamie and at one time she earned a living working with them, caring for a stable of expensive horses, doing some horse training for others, and she now trains her own barrel horses. Ironically, at one point she was training a granddaughter of Pally who she first ran 17 years before!

It seems strange for me now, as I think back, to ever have thought that the unusual happens only to others. For years, I was often told, by veterinarians and doctors mostly but even other folks, that things that happened to or with me were so unusual that the term "only, you, Joan" became common. Because even after years of those types of experiences, I learned the hard way adverse things don't happen just to others.

For years I had premonitions of "the call" I would get sometime in the middle of the night. It would tell me my son, Scott, had been in a terrible accident and was dead. I got that call on January 20, 1991 just as I had feared – only it was to tell me his best friend, Ed, whom he'd been riding four-wheelers with that night, was dead on arrival at the hospital in Titusville and Scott was in St. Vincent's hospital in Erie. While I mourned for Ed, I was relieved my son was still alive.

The first thing I did was to call our dear friends Wes and Marge Aarum to pray for him and for us and then we went down the road to get our daughter in law. Michael then eight, and Jamie six, were taken to their aunt Laura Lee's while Michelle went with us to the hospital. My heart was breaking for Melanie, Ed's wife, and for his children, as I knew they were probably even then finding out about their husband/father. When we arrived at the hospital and identified ourselves, they told us Scott was being given a cat scan and we would have to wait to see him.

As we sat in the room waiting for the opportunity to do so, the story of the accident began to unfold. It seems the men, three of them, were riding their four-wheelers on the icy back roads after having had been to a local bar where they had been drinking. One individual with them was not invited; Scott and Ed didn't want him with them and tried to "lose" him by going ahead without him to their friend Mark's house. Mark normally would have been riding with them but refused to go because he was concerned about an accident occurring.

Scott and Ed left Mark's and headed back toward the little town of Lincolnville. Leaving Mark's, the road goes down a steep hill with a short, narrow bridge at the bottom, the road then ascending to the top of the other side of the hill, each side about as steep as the other. The bridge at the bottom was a one-lane bridge with steel guard rails and a deck made out of heavy steel mesh.

The facts remain obscure to this day, and many theories spawned as people reflected on the incident, but no one knows exactly what transpired on that hill that fateful night. What is known is that Scott and Ed were traveling down the hill from the west, Ed being a bit behind Scott. An acquaintance, Greg, was traveling east down the other side. Scott and Greg collided head on and Scott was thrown headfirst into the bridge. He was not wearing a helmet. Greg came off his wheeler as well, but it continued to travel until it slammed into Ed on his. Ed was ejected from his machine. What was soon discovered was that one man was dead, one was seriously injured, and the other had suffered a broken leg.

Another part of the story began to unfold as we waited there in that hospital. I was in touch with our other son, Randy, by phone as he had called the hospital looking for us. Randy had gone to Titusville after talking to Mark who had been one of the first on the scene from the beginning, living just a few hundred yards from the accident. While Randy was trying to relate something to me a nurse came in asking if Scott had any identifying marks. We told her he had a tattoo. Something didn't compute all of a sudden to me. I asked for silence in the room and told all there that I think Randy and the nurse are trying to tell us something.

They were and it was just as I had suspected. It was Ed in the emergency room in the hospital where we waited and it was my son who was DOA at another hospital, thirty miles away.

As soon as we realized the truth, I asked about Ed's wife, Melanie, and discovered she was also in this same hospital as she had known the truth before we did. I asked the nurse to find her and let her know we would like to see her. We wanted her to know we were concerned, and we would be praying for them all. The nurse returned and told us Melanie was reluctant to see us. I then asked the nurse to assure her we were not angry in any way and just wanted to comfort them if possible. She then agreed.

We met Melanie along with Ed's father, Bob, just outside the room we had been waiting in. We had known Ed for years but had never met Bob before. We all told them how sorry we were for Ed's injuries – by now we knew he was in a coma – and that we would pray for his recovery. This was very early Sunday morning. At the first viewing for Scott on Monday, we were approached by the preacher of the church in Lincolnville (the little town closest to the accident site and also the town in which Ed's father lived). He told us that Ed's father had accepted Jesus Christ as his Savior that Sunday afternoon after he had seen God's love evidenced in our lives in the midst of our tragedy. Ed remained in a coma for several weeks, but gradually his condition improved and after many months returned to a fairly normal life.

Afraid of the emotional aspect of the entire funeral process and sure I would never endure it, I was amazed once again by the grace of God. As we entered the funeral home for the first and private showing for family only, I stood in the vestibule and told Bill I couldn't go in and see him. I asked him, "How am I going to get through this?" Nothing in the entire world was important that day as I realized the fragility of life. I struggled feeling I wouldn't even be able to enter the room where our son was laid, but God saw my helpless state and intervened. He gave me the strength to not only enter the room and stand by the casket, but I later found myself comforting others who came to comfort us. Oh, I learned much about the grace of God during those times as only God could provide the strength and comfort I so needed.

Chapter Twenty-Nine

HE DIDN'T TAKE HER

Proverbs 9:11: "For by me your days will be multiplied, and years of life will be added to you." (NKJV)

Pocobud was a beautiful palomino mare who had two foals prior to this one. The first two were palomino also and very pretty – this was a red colt, and he was a cutie. I was right with her when she foaled and while foaling seemed to go normally, shortly afterward it became apparent things were not natural. The mare seemed to be in great distress, not just acting "off" a bit, but in acute pain. I was scared and called the vet immediately.

Rick Orosko from Camboro Veterinary Hospital was the one who came to treat her. We walked out into the little pasture where the mare had foaled and looked her over. Rick could not find anything conclusive to pin the symptoms on and treated her with what he felt best at the time. We watched her for a bit as she settled down considerably then we made our way back to the barn where he had parked his truck.

As we approached the barn Rick asked my permission to pray for the mare. I was dumbstruck! As a Christian I was certainly interested in praying for my horse, but to have my veterinarian ask to pray for her was astounding. I readily and most wholeheartedly agreed. We stood in front of the barn while Rick prayed; asking God to spare the mare and make her well then prepared to leave. After prayer and further instructions, we parted. We had done all we could.

As he got into his truck and I started to walk to the house, we both noticed Pocobud lying down – flat out. We both changed course and went back to check on her, both thinking she may have died. She was okay – only resting. Whew! After a short time, she got up from where she was sleeping and seemed perfectly normal. We praised God for sparing her, and ultimately her foal's life.

All seemed fine. Eight weeks went by and mother and son were doing well. They were turned out with Pocobud's mother, her full sister, and another mare making a total of four mares with their foals.

I was off to a barrel racing clinic not too far from home. In the early afternoon I received a call from Bill's cousin, Tammy, who was staying at our home for the weekend. Something was wrong with Pocobud. I had her call the vet to get him out there immediately and promise to keep me informed of his findings. He came and I was subsequently called to come home.

When I got there, Tom Allen, the attending vet was waiting for me. He had been examining Pocobud and was unable to find a cause for her symptoms. She had something horrible going on and had become violent in her pain. She was throwing herself around, into anything and anyone, unaware of her surroundings: She was falling and thrashing while down. The only thing evident was that something was terribly wrong and the mare was not far from death. Tom explained he could not save her and anything he did would only prolong the pain for her. He asked permission to euthanize her. I looked at the frantic colt in the stall next to her who had never been separated from her for a moment. He was too young to lose his mother, but what could I do? Reluctantly I made the decision that ended her suffering.

Titan, her foal, had been housed in a stall next to her while all this was going on and now we had to turn our attention to him. He had never been in a barn, never been separated from the other mares and foals. After exploring the possibilities of his care it was decided to return him to the pasture with the others. We had a creep feed (a place where foals could be fed, that the mothers could not access) in their barn for the foals and he had been using it. There was a good chance he would continue to eat. I would keep an eye on him and see if he would survive better out there. More traumas to him in a stall would not be helpful to his emotional or physical wellbeing.

Lying in bed that night I was overcome with grief at the loss of this beautiful and special mare. With tears in my eyes I said to Bill: "Why did God take Pocobud?" I shall never forget his immediate and factual response, largely due to the fact that such a response was totally out of character for Bill and I knew the answer was coming from my heavenly Father. He said: "Joan, God didn't take Pocobud. He let her stay here long enough to let that colt make it without her." I was amazed by the answer. He was right! The mare could have died the day the foal was born, and the colt wouldn't have had much of a chance in those days without her. God let her stay until her son could live without her.

Tom told me that while watching Titan over the next weeks I should understand that Titan will grieve for a period and then should pick up and move on. I watched him mope and whinny for his mom and it broke my heart. I forced myself not to interfere for that week or so it took and was amazed that just over one week from the time he lost his mom, he seemed to pick up his head, look the world in the eye, and move on! He was okay and going to make it. I had him until he died at almost 28 years old, and in his 27th year he carried me to a team roping rodeo win and a friend to a buckle for an entire winter of barrel racing. He's one of the few horses that we never sold.

Scott could have very easily been killed many times previous to that cold night in January, 1991. In many instances it was nothing short of a miracle he wasn't. But God, in His infinite wisdom said, "It is not time, yet." Just like that mare, it was too early. None of us were ready to make it without him. God let him stay until He knew we could. Just as God provided for that colt, won't He much more provide for Scott's son, his daughter, wife, brother, sister, mother, father? He loves us much more than a colt.

No, God didn't take Scott. He let him stay.

Chapter Thirty

THE TERRIBLE TWOS

*Psalm 25:17: "The troubles of my heart have enlarged; oh, bring me out of my distresses!"
(NKJV)*

The terrible twos started with the death of my mother in 1989. I had been in Canada with Wes and Marge Aarum singing in a crusade for two weeks. My mother was in a mental health facility for the second time with a nervous breakdown. While in Canada I stayed with a couple by the name of Abe and Catherine Thiessen. They both worked during the day and I had some sweet time alone. I used some of that time to learn a new song I had discovered and brought along for that very reason. I had no intention of singing it while there as it was new to me and I had already had my numbers selected. I did end up singing it on Sunday morning – the last day I was there. I sang it for a new friend I'd met who needed encouraged by its comforting words. I had no idea the impact it would have on me personally – or how soon.

The next day I flew back arriving home on Monday night. Mother was in the hospital in the mental health ward where she had been for a week or so and visitors were not permitted. She was to get out in a day or two. I had purchased a couple of encouraging books and another small gift for her and planned on going to see her on Friday to spend the afternoon with her. I had too many things to catch up on to go earlier and she would need to get home and settle in first anyway.

Friday came. It was mid-morning when my mother called me on the phone. She was calling to let me know of a couple of people from her church not too much older than she was (mother was 73) that had died. We talked about them and then some family news. She then let me know she was a little miffed because she hadn't seen me yet. I told her of my plans to come in and spend the afternoon with her and that I had gotten her a couple of things. She said she was glad to hear that as she told me, "I won't be around forever, you know". Those were pretty much her last words to me. About an hour and a half later I got a call from my sister telling me my mother was dead. She had died of a heart attack brought on by congestive heart failure. Had I been any less secure in my relationship with her, her words would likely have haunted me the rest of my life. However, I knew I had shown her my love and spent more time with her than anyone else in the family and that she had only been upset for the moment.

Two years later we lost our son, Scott, in the four-wheeler accident described earlier. Those were very dark days. Because I was the designated bearer of bad news, I was chosen to tell our grandchildren their father was never coming home. I will never forget that moment. It was one of the hardest moments of my life. The children were asking me when their father would be coming home and I had to watch the dreadful moments that followed as they crumpled under the weight of the news. Life will never be the same for many of us without him. He has been missed each and every day since.

Life is full of reminders of this loss. Just the other day, while looking something up in one of my Bibles, I came across a "book" my grandson, Michael, wrote about six weeks after his dad died. It is just a few slips of paper and has very few words, but it speaks volumes. "Scott Vincent Wurst, Mike, Dad, 1991, Saturday. My dad died in a four-wheeler accident – he was the strongest man. He liked to rope. He said that I was going to be his heeling partner. But I wasn't." Every time it is read by me or to others, it evokes intense emotions in each as we are reminded of that painful, life changing event.

Another difficult thing I had to do was go to Bill, lying on the bed sobbing, and tell him we needed to stick together on this, to talk about it, and be there for one another or it would destroy our marriage. For most of our lives together to that point, it wouldn't have taken much to destroy our marriage and I feared this would be the situation that would do so. We were still in the beginning stages of communication and trusting God for our responses to each other and I was fearful the outcome might not be good. By God's grace he responded to that need and we talked freely about the situation from that moment on. It was good for both of us.

I would sit on our couch, facing the little cemetery beyond the woods and a field just two miles away where Scott lays, and I would wonder how I could go on another moment. Then I would think of all the women who lost their beloved children, especially those with time on their hands (which I had none of, always being busy), and those who didn't know the Lord as I did, and I wondered how they endured life at all. Many times I thought it would be easier to just go ahead and lose my mind as maybe that would take the unbearable pain away.

Just weeks after losing Scott, I traveled to Manitoba, Canada to fulfill a singing obligation. It was so hard to go to a place where I knew very few people and put on a happy face but even in that difficult trip, I found God way ahead of me. The first new people I met had lost not one, not two, but three sons! I then met others who had lost children and we cried together. They were such a comfort to my soul as I could share my grief with others who truly understood the pain of this ultimate loss.

In just another two years we were challenged again with big losses. In July of 1993, Bill's youngest brother succumbed to an illness. Only a few weeks after that tragedy our two precious grandchildren Scott had given us were taken from us when their mom and her new husband moved to Mississippi. Losing those children in this way was like two more deaths in my life. Not long after their departure my father died unexpectedly. He had gone into the hospital with pneumonia and thought he had gotten there in time, giving us all assurance he would be okay. He died of a heart attack that night. His death occurred just a few days before our annual rodeo was to be held. It was too late to even attempt to cancel it, so we held the viewing off to begin the day after the rodeo. It was an emotionally taxing time. These three losses all took place within a six-week period.

My mother had gotten very angry at my sister, Kathy, years before when she moved to Texas taking my mother's two favorite grandchildren with her. At the time I thought she was grossly overreacting to the situation. I understand her reaction now. When it happened to me it opened my eyes to her pain. It was terrible contemplating the loss up to the day they left, but that day was agonizingly painful. The kids hung unto me, wailing, and I fought as hard as I could to keep from doing the same. A piece of me died as they left the drive, the ranch, and the life they loved behind. Michael cried so hard for so long, they considered hospitalizing him.

I prayed and cried to the Lord for some sort of consolation. He directed me to a verse in Jeremiah wherein it states: "…and they shall come back from the land …there is hope in your future, says the Lord that your children shall come back to their own border." How I was to hang onto those verses for the hope they would return. About a year and a half later, I received a letter from Michael. Not prone to writing, it was very short, but oh, what a message it had. It said simply, "Jeremiah 29:14. Read it. Yours truly Mik" (Mik is my pet nickname for him.) The verse reads, "I will be found by you, says the Lord, and I will bring you back from your captivity." (NKJV) I had never shared with anyone but Bill the promise of that verse yet God in His mercy gave Michael the same promise to comfort him while we were apart. A long five years later, they moved back to our area.

Two more years flew by and we ran into some severe business problems that more than drained us financially and emotionally. We bid a large water line installation scheduled to begin early in the spring. We reasoned this job would keep us going until weather was conducive to moving dirt and hauling gravel, the two things we did the most of, and made the most profit doing. When it was discovered there was a delay in the start of the job we bid, and got, a smaller utility job, assuming and planning on getting it done right away. We would then go to the larger job, and still be in good shape for summer work.

As things go, neither of the jobs started when scheduled. They were delayed so long (governmental hang ups) that when they did start, they both required us to be working on them at the same time. In addition the weather changed, was good, and several dirt jobs needed to be done as well. We did not have enough in the way of supervisors and even enough equipment to handle that many jobs. We did what we thought best at the time which was the best we could do. One thing we did was hire another utility contractor to oversee and run some of his equipment on one of the utility installation jobs. It didn't work out as it should have or as we expected and the job ran way over estimated time and expense. It cost us dearly.

On another job, again with someone supposed to be well-qualified for the position, an accident occurred that caused an employee to lose several fingers and sustain extensive damage to his hand. The employee had his hand resting on the pipe in the ditch when the excavator operator dropped the bucket of the machine onto it. On top of his misfortune that incident cost us a great deal of money on the job as well as our Worker's Compensation Carrier. By the time the year was over we had lost more than the company was worth. The following year we lost another considerable sum as the effects of the previous year continued.

And two years later we were to discover most of Bill's unexplained physical problems he had been troubled with for some time were the result of Lyme Disease. He was in such poor health that in May of 2000, the year of our 40th wedding anniversary, we had a ceremony renewing our vows. We did this as we weren't sure he would make it to 50 years. We did want to renew them at some point as they meant more to us now than they did so long ago as children. God provided answers and good medical help for Bill and we made it very close to 56 years of marriage.

Many more "terrible's" didn't come quite in two's, but come they did.

Chapter Thirty-One

SINGING

Psalm 104:33: "I will sing to the Lord as long as I live; I will sing praise to my God while I have my being." (NKJV)

I always loved to sing, yet I was always too self-conscious to sing in front of anyone unless I was singing with a group of people and could fade out if I didn't feel I could reach a note or get the harmony correctly. I dreamed of having a singing career, but then I loved to dream even when I knew the things I dreamed about would never come true.

Bill needed calves for practice roping but we could not afford to buy them old enough to use immediately so we would buy three-day old calves from a farmer and I would bottle feed and raise them until they were old enough to be roped. We would then use them until they got too big to rope any longer at which time we would take them to the auction, sell them and use that money to buy more calves.

Calves that young do better with nurturing and time spent with them and we needed them to do well. It took a considerable amount of time to bottle or bucket feed them and I used that time to sing to them. It gave me an outlet for and seemed to have a relaxing effect on the calves. They grew and did very well for me.

In his later years, my uncle Ray had a friend, Smokey, who had at one point in his life played guitar in Marty Robbin's band. Somewhere along the line, Uncle Ray had heard me sing and he encouraged me to pursue a career in singing. Knowing how I felt about even attempting to sing in front of anyone he would try to entice me to go to the tavern with him. He said if I would drink a few beers, I would not be afraid to sing. I may have considered it if not for the strict upbringing I had had, the resultant sense of right and wrong, and the intense teaching of the perils of alcohol. I really wanted to be a well-known singer but I did not go to the tavern and many years went by before I ever sang in public.

When we moved to the new property we met neighbors (1 mile away) and now had new friends. Sandy & Stanley Allen sang often with their children in church but most often the two of them sang duets. Learning of my love for singing, they encouraged me to sing with them. It took some time but eventually I allowed my strong desire to sing to overcome my fears just enough to give it a try. It was so intimidating I could only sing quietly and let them drown me out with their voices. It took years to gain enough confidence to progress to singing a duet with one of them at a time and even more years to sing a solo.

After singing solo for a short time, I decided to quit. It was just too hard emotionally to place myself in such a vulnerable position. I totally lacked any confidence in my ability to sing and it showed in my voice. The only thing that kept me going at all was the fact that Sandy & Stanley had a daughter, Lois, who played the piano and could play songs an octave lower than written. This worked for me as I have a low voice and limited range. She was my answer to singing with a little more confidence: At least I did not have to strain so hard to hit the notes.

Just after beginning to get a small measure of confidence to sing with Lois's help, Sandy, Stanley, and family moved away. Here I was just getting started and now I was sure that would end my short-lived desire. I had no recourse for back up now.

I felt once again it was the end of my singing career and I was devastated. Now, not wanting to give up, I searched for other ways to enable me to continue singing and was eventually introduced to accompaniment tracts. I was warned they could be tricky to sing to but I was determined to try. Learning to work with them opened up a whole new world of singing for me. Still the songs with range available for me to use were very limited. (Now the machines that change the key without distorting the music have enabled me to have a much broader repertoire.)

In each case, when I thought God was allowing my opportunities to sing to be lost, he opened new and better possibilities. It was never the end, but a bright new beginning. (If God closes a door, He opens a window.)

Gaining confidence did not come easy though. I would sing and be so frightened before, during, and even after that it was just getting too hard for me to deal with. I was just about convinced to quit altogether and forever when I talked to a friend about it. She has a beautiful voice and seemed to have all the confidence she needed to sing to an audience. I was surprised to find out she felt the same way as I did. That did not help me at all.

In an effort to decide what the right thing to do was, I began to talk to the Lord about it. Did He want me to quit? Through this search, God began to speak to me about why I was singing. He made me realize that while I thought I was singing for Him, by being so afraid of what others might think of me, I was actually singing more for myself. I told Him I wanted to change that and if He would show me that even one person was touched or reached by my singing, then I would continue and I would be grateful for that one. From that time on, I sang for Him and He has never let me down.

He has given me confirmation each time as needed. He also used this situation to help me realize that my life needed to be spent pleasing Him, not others, and not by being so concerned about myself. This development also helped me realize my life does not depend upon everyone liking me. God was showing me it was okay if everyone did not like my singing. He was interested in the one who did respond to it enough for Him to reach through me.

While spending all that time at Circle C Ranch, Wes Aarum learned of my love for singing and graciously encouraged me to sing at some of the services held at the ranch. I was petrified and as a result probably not very good, but he continued to give me opportunity. To illustrate my ignorance about music, I will never forget the incident when a group of us were practicing for just such a service. Wes was trying to discover which key I needed a song played in so they could accompany me with various instruments. He was going to accompany me on the piano and Ron Snell would accompany on the guitar. Ron asked me what key I needed. I told him I did not know what key it would be on the guitar but it was G on the piano. They got a good laugh and I almost died from embarrassment.

Bill and I became very good friends with Wes and his wife, Marge. After gaining enough confidence to sing in front of others, we traveled with them to some evangelistic services where I provided the special music. Those were special times of fellowship along with spiritual and emotional growth.

During a trip to Manitoba on a crusade with Wes and Marge I was privileged to meet a wonderful family, that of Frank and Alfreda Dyck. Frank was just recovering from open heart surgery and was not feeling his best. It was at his church that I was to sing the final time before leaving for home. As I said, I had my songs picked out, but I felt a prompting to take this new number with me, and so I did. When I got to the church, I gave the sound man my two selections. After further consideration I gave him the third song as well; the new one. I told him I would let him know which to play for me when the time came. I sang my first number and when it was time for my second, I told the folks I felt impressed to sing a brand new song entitled "God On The Mountain." I sang it and Frank was sure it was sung specifically for him. I agreed as I was sure he was right.

My mother's death came just days after returning home from that trip and upon being told she had died, almost my first thoughts were the words of that song that I had so recently learned; "for the God on the mountain, is the God in the valley, when things go wrong, He'll make them right, and *the God of the good times, is the God of the bad times, the God of the day, is the God of the night.* I was comforted by those words and overwhelmed at the thought that God had taught me that song to prepare me to hear from Him during this very difficult time. Once again He was so far ahead of me!

After singing with soundtracks long enough to be comfortable with them I was told by some full time professional singers that in order to be any kind of a success I would have to be able to write songs. I would not get anywhere by only singing someone else's, they said. Well, that squelched my career once again! Now I was sure it was the end of it all. Years before I had attempted a poem and a song and did not feel either was worth anything. I would not be able to do it. It was beyond my reach.

The day after my mother died, my older sister asked me what her favorite poem was so we could read it at her funeral. For the life of me I could not remember it, nor could she. We both knew well it was "Footsteps" and both recalled it easily a couple of days later. But at the time nothing came to either of us. I had never written a poem; the only thing I had ever written was a short story for a high school class assignment.

Wanting a poem for her funeral, in my grief I sat down and wrote one – a personal one for her. – saying what I thought she might want to say to us. It was relatively easy. The next morning, prepared to go teach my Sunday school class I was overcome with grief once more and could not leave the house. I sat and wrote another poem. I liked it as well. They are included at the conclusion of this chapter.

Marge and Wes Aarum came to visit and console me and I shared the poems with them. Wes, who majored in music, said they were good poems and he felt I should begin writing lyrics to put to music. That encouragement led me to begin writing songs, eventually leading to recording an album of all originals. At that time the songs I wrote were written out of the emotional pain I was living in and I entitled the album "In Memory Of", in honor of my son, Scott. Each song I wrote has ministered to me more than anyone else.

No one has ever been more amazed at the ability to do these things than I am! God is responsible for all and He amazes me at what He has done through me, just the vessel.

Weep Not
Weep not for me my loved ones,
As I cross the crystal sea;
For Jesus will bear me safely over,
To the place He has prepared for me.

No more I'll suffer pain or strife,
As was my lot down here;
For now I'll live in joy forever,
With my Savior, Dear.

I'll be in that peaceful valley,
I've longed for, oh so long.
I'll sing in the heavenly choir,
Around the Master's throne.

So weep not for me, my loved ones,
For my life has just begun.
The final battle's over,
And victory has been won.
© Joan E. Wurst
Remember
Remember not those times in life,
When I would unfair be.
For cares of life would cause such strife
That only me, I'd see.

Remember not, as years went by
Those unkind things I'd say,
But look instead to reasons why,
I changed from day to day.

Remember not the times I'd fall,
The wrong things that I'd do;
Remember instead, in spite of all,
I had great love for you.

Remember me, as I will Thee,
Remember me, and yet.
Remember not those things of me,
That I'd like to forget.

© Joan E. Wurst

Chapter Thirty-Two

THE SKELETON IN THE CLOSET

Psalm 139:13: "For you created my inmost being; you knit me together in my mother's womb." (NIV)

They say we all have one. The one I uncovered was to send me reeling for most of my life.

I was 19, living in that awful apartment with two babies. My aunt Helen, my mother's sister, had helped me get groceries this one particular day and we returned 'home' with them. We were climbing the steep stairs to the kitchen, she a step or two above me, when from out of nowhere she says to me, "Joe isn't your father, you know. Robert is." I almost fell back down the stairs! I was so shocked I do not remember to this day any further conversation about it at the time. Other than me telling my husband what she had said, it remained in the back of my mind but was not brought up again for over 25 years. There was only one other mention of Robert and a relationship with me. That was when Bill's father made the remark that I must have had an affair with Robert as, according to him, our son, Randy, looked just like him. The idea angered me but there was no sense in trying to change his mind or convince him otherwise. I had to bite my tongue and let it go. Thinking the way they did about me his parents must have been so disappointed in Bill's poor choice for a mate. How hard it must have been for them to watch what they thought was the destruction of their favorite son.

After attending a Bible conference meeting many years later, a group of us stopped at a local restaurant to "fellowship". As we sat at the table, I was sitting next to my sister, Jean. Once again I was blindsided when she turned to me and said something about Robert being my father! "Where did that come from?" I thought. She had never even insinuated anything relating to the subject previously. This was not a good place to talk about it so I made contact with her shortly after that to see what she knew.

In our conversation about the matter, I discovered that several relatives knew (or thought they knew) about it and had for years. No one talked about it to me but they did to each other. Supposedly it was true. While my mother never admitted it to anyone, her sister was convinced of the truth. My aunt Helen claimed she observed revealing behavior between them and asked my mother outright at one point if I was Robert's child. My mother had an extreme aversion to lying and when asked that demanding question did not deny, but responded with, "You'll never hear it from these lips". That was proof enough for her sister. I was dumfounded with this entire revelation. The biggest issue for me at first was realizing, if this was true, I was an only child in a sense. Due to my mother's half siblings not seeming like her sisters and brothers at all, I had always had an aversion to the relationship. Oh, I did not dislike any of my half-aunts and half uncles – they were among my better friends. They just did not seem like my mother's siblings. Now here I was with nine half brothers and sisters and not a full brother or sister at all! The sisters and brothers I knew as mine all my life thus far were in a sense, not. I felt yet another great loss and I was heartsick.

I so wanted the truth but my mother had died shortly before I had to face this and I did not want to approach my father with it in case he did not know. Why tarnish the memory of his wife if he had no idea of this indiscretion? I could not hurt him that way. I agonized over wanting the truth.

Many things confirmed the rumor to be true in my eyes. I look very much like one of Robert's daughters, nothing like any on my mother's side. I have several of his characteristics evident in my life. Our oldest son, Randy is very much like this man in many ways. Some things like these are apparent. There was so much circumstantial evidence substantiating the claim that proof was not really necessary. I knew the truth.

A doctor friend told me I should go to the trouble to find the truth for certain as health concerns for me and my children could be totally opposite with the two different fathers. He was right, as there was a whole different set of issues with each. I guess I did need to know for sure, but how to do so? He suggested I get a DNA sample of my blood done and then try to find a way to get one from the father who raised me. The problem with that is it could not be done without his consent and I would not lie to him nor for reasons stated above did I want to talk to him about it. It seemed I was at a dead end. I did get a DNA sample of my blood which was stored by the testing lab so it would be available should the opportunity ever arise in which I would be able to get my dad's.

In his eighties, my father began having problems with pneumonia and was hospitalized with it a couple of times. The last time he went in was in the summer of 1993. I spoke to him on the phone at about 8:00 in the evening of the day he was admitted. My sister, Jean, was the one who took him to the hospital and stayed with him, as her home was only a few hundred feet from his and they were almost twenty miles closer to the hospital. In our conversation he sounded good and said he was sure they got him there on time as all the tests showed a good supply of oxygen to the blood. He was in great spirits and I was relieved. I loved this man. Before hanging up I assured him I would be in to see him the next day. It was just a few days before our rodeo and I was up to my neck in busyness but I would make time.

The opportunity never presented itself as Jean called around midnight to tell me he had just died. I spoke to her for a few minutes and hung up the phone with nothing going through my mind but the realization he was gone. A few moments later the phone rang again – again it was Jean. She told me they were going to do an autopsy on our father to determine the exact cause of death and did I want a blood sample to get a DNA match done? Did I? This was my chance after all! What an answer to prayer and I had almost missed the last opportunity I would have. Arrangements were made but there was a small obstacle. The hospital staff informed us that since my father could not give permission for the test the executor of his estate would have to sign for it. That meant I had to tell my oldest brother about it and ask him to do so. Jim had lived out of state since he was 18 years old and entered the service. We seldom even saw him. I had no idea how he would react to the request knowing what it inferred about our mother. With the exception of my children and a few very close friends, I had never talked to anyone about this situation and at this point I was very reluctant to let anyone else know about it. I explained as little as I could to my brother, who seemed very unconcerned and asked no questions. The two of us made the trip to the hospital where he signed the consent form. This was in the middle of August.

I was sure what the outcome of the DNA testing would be. And even though it was on my mind much of the time I was sure I would not feel much one way or the other about it. After all I had *known* the truth for some time, hadn't I? About six weeks after the test was taken, the report did come in with the regular mail one day and was brought to me in my office downstairs. With three other offices next to mine and several girls working in them I closed the door to have some privacy.

I sat and contemplated the large white envelope in my hands for some time. This item, this envelope, contained the facts of my origin. I stared at it. Once I opened it and read its contents there would be no mystery, no speculation, and no questions remaining. Those who had questioned me for so long could finally be silenced one way or the other. On one hand I was anxious to finally know the truth – on the other I was reluctant to know at all. I slowly opened the envelope and pulled out the report it contained. Helpless now it seemed to wait any longer I skimmed through the explanations to the bottom line. Here, finally was the truth. I could put to rest all the doubting and wondering. My thoughts raced: What would I do if Joe was my father after all and all these circumstantial proofs were wrong? What would I do if he weren't my father? I would cross each bridge as I got to it, I mused. As my eyes reached the line with the final fact of the matter, they settled on the statement that plainly read: "Joe Wasiela is not your biological father."

Convinced as I was before reading it that I would only find confirmation of what I already knew I did not expect the feelings that flooded my mind. I was totally unprepared for my reaction. I began to tremble and I cried. It broke my heart. To me it tore my family apart. The truth of no full brothers and sisters, the knowledge I had other brothers and sisters who didn't know I was their sister, the man I loved as a father was not my father, how could my mother never tell me; all these things flooded into my head and filtered to my heart.

After a time of recovering from the initial shock, I was now faced with what to do with the information I had before me. I needed time to think.

One of my brothers began asking me about the results even before I had received them as he was one that had heard about it years before. Yet even after I got them, I could not bring myself to tell him and just hedged around his questions. All of a sudden this was an extremely private matter. I didn't even reveal the contents of the report to Jean for some time. When I did, I asked her not to divulge the information to anyone else.

I did tell my children and thought about others who might have reason to know. One of the most astounding facts about the situation was that Bev, my lifelong close friend, the one for whom I had been Matron of Honor in her wedding, the one who had been like a sister to me, *was* my sister! Our similarities in appearance were no mistake as it turns out – it was reasonable that we look alike when it was discovered we shared the same biological father. I needed to tell her. I was anxious about the thought of doing so, fearful of her reaction. After all this was going to be quite a shock to her and it was not a compliment to her father. People might say in his defense that he was not married at the time, however, that doesn't make it right and while I can understand my mother's loneliness and other emotional needs at that period of her life, she was married with three children at the time of their indiscretion.

Bev and I hadn't seen much of each other for several years prior to this revelation as while I was so busy with all things going on in my life, she and her husband were also busy building a home, small farm, and a veterinary practice about an hour away. It was quite a surprise when she showed up on my doorstep just a few days after the revealing mail had. We made small talk and I told her I had something important to discuss with her. That in itself was not unusual as we had shared many things over the years. Not knowing a better way to begin, I asked her how she would feel if she was to discover she had another sister. After the initial surprise of such a question, she replied: "I guess it would depend upon who it was." I said, "What if it was me?" Without hesitation she responded with, "I'd be honored". How I loved her for that and how grateful I was to have that huge obstacle out of the way for me.

After a long discussion about the matter, we decided not to tell anyone for the time being. Like the situation with my father, we didn't want to hurt her mother. It was not an easy thing to do. For one thing, people that know both Bev and me are always asking if we are sisters. Others who see us ask if we are sisters. We were put in difficult situations as we didn't want to lie about anything. I just wanted to get the issue out in the open and have some closure to it.

Babies can acquire things, even while in the womb, from things done or said around them. Add to that infants can pick up on things no one suspected so long ago. I wonder to this day if things were said around me pertaining to this situation and that was why I always felt out of place and different in my family.

I keep asking myself what my mother must have thought and felt like spending all that time with me (far more than any of her other children), knowing the truth, and knowing I did not. Did she ever want to tell me? How could she not? Agonizing over that thought I tried to put myself in her place and figure out the answers to those questions. Of course I couldn't know, but I believe I might have some insight. The most obvious reason I suppose would be the shame of it all and how I might feel about her. I imagine she might have thought of what it could do to me, as well as her husband, to find out the man I loved as my father was not my father at all. What purpose would it serve to sever any relationships over it? What reasoning could dictate causing pain to any of us over something that was irreversible? If I was in her shoes, I wonder if I would ever have said anything either, especially while my husband was alive. Perhaps she might have told me some day if things had happened differently, but as she died before her husband, that never happened.

Even after all this there were still one or two people that brought up the point that even though my mother's husband was not my father, it didn't prove Robert was. Was I sure? As I mentioned before, the circumstantial evidence is overwhelming, especially that Bev and I look enough alike that at one point even my four-year-old grandson was calling her Grandma from about 30 feet away. Aside from a common parent it would be just about impossible for us to look that much alike. Even though I had absolutely no doubt, it was very unsettling to have others still doubting it. It gave me no chance for closure on the subject. It was irritating and exasperating. I decided to try to go one-step further in my proof and planned to pay Robert a visit. I told no one of my plan.

It was difficult to find him by himself and it was months later when the opportunity to talk to him finally came. I was making a trip home from Erie and took a chance of finding him home alone. I stopped by and found him there, working in his garage. We chitchatted for a couple of moments and then I told him the real reason I was there. I told him what I had discovered about the father who had raised me and I needed to hear from him directly that he was my father. He promptly told me he couldn't do that as he could not possibly be my father. He used his time in the service to substantiate the fact that he couldn't have been here, but I had done some homework as well, and reminded him that he had been home that February in 1942.

That out of the way, he began making other forms of denial until I said to him: "Okay, you say you are not my father. Then you have to help me find out who is. You know how close our families have always been and you know everyone who my parents knew and mostly what they were doing. I have nowhere else to look and neither does anyone else. If it was not you, then you tell me where to go look. I have a right to know who my father is and I need a name. Oh, and by the way, if you're not my father, get a DNA test to prove it and I'll leave you alone about it." At this he became noticeably subdued, albeit quite nervous, and after a moment quietly revealed to me that he had been close enough to my mother for me to be his child. That revelation did give relief knowing the question was finally answered. It also provided a measure of closure to not have to search for the truth any longer. He begged me to keep it to myself. He explained he did not want his wife hurt over the situation. Outside of the few that already knew, I did. At least at some future point I felt I might have the opportunity to bring this out in the open and eliminate all the cloak and dagger avoidances of the truth.

One of the most difficult things about being aware of this situation was listening to Robert brag about his grandchildren; the first one, the one who flies, the one who likes equipment, etc. when both of us knew my children were his first grandchildren and my grandchildren were his first great grandchildren. I was able to have a picture taken with him, my granddaughter, and great granddaughter shortly before he died. It is the only picture of the five generations ever taken, even though Scott was missing. To have these things never acknowledged is still a sore spot.

Robert died before Jill. This put Bev and I in the same situation I had been with the man I knew as my father growing up. Did she know? Again, we reached the same conclusion– leave it alone until she was gone so we don't take a chance of hurting her. I felt awful every time I was around one of my three other siblings who didn't know who I really was. I felt like a traitor. Jill went home to be with the Lord in the early Spring one year and Bev made the decision to tell the other three when they were together, taking care of their parent's possessions. It was received with mixed emotions I am told.

My sister, Bonnie, was justifiably hurt and a bit angry at being kept in the dark about it for so long. I finally explained to her what the situation had done to me all my life and how I had made the promises to others in her family for their sake and had to keep those promises. She understood better after that and became one of my biggest allies. I had always had a love for Bonnie and had secretly hoped I looked a lot like her when she was a teenager.

One of my brothers on that side didn't comment much at all – and hasn't to this day, although is as friendly to me as ever. I don't know what he thinks about it all. The other one asked a logical question of Bev when he said, "how do we know it was dad?" It only made sense one might ask that, even with the strong circumstantial evidence, but it really bothered me. What was he trying to say about my mother? I was trying so hard to get closure with this thing and seemed to keep running into roadblocks. Due to his question and the ones from my side as well, Bev and I decided to go the final step and check our DNA for siblings. We told no one of our actions until the results came back. When they did, It proved beyond a shadow of a doubt that we are, indeed, sisters. Presenting that truth to my brother sealed the issue and he has been wonderfully supportive of me – beginning to introduce me to his children and grandchildren as their aunt. This situation has to be difficult for those grown children of my siblings. All of a sudden to have the family friend their relative.

I struggled with much of this, I felt somehow this entire situation was my fault and yet realistically, I knew that couldn't be true. It still bothered me for some time until I allowed my heavenly Father to convince me of the truth. I had nothing to do with it.

Chapter Thirty-Three

UNMET DESIRES AND SPECIAL GIFTS

James 1:17: "Every good and perfect is from above, and comes down from the Father." (NKJV)

You've probably guessed by now that I love animals. In my early years of marriage, I raised and showed Saint Bernards for a period, which was something I enjoyed immensely. In addition to that, I started the Presque Isle Saint Bernard Club and was involved in it for years. I have shown only one dog in obedience. He was a Saint Bernard and I got a Companion Dog title on him in the least number of shows possible. Contrary to public opinion, Saints can make good obedience performers; this one having taken honors for highest score of all breeds in a match at one point. I believe the dogs, as with the horses, were a great source of emotional fulfillment and helped my self esteem.

The unconditional love of the dogs and having them to love without fear of rejection filled an important part of my life. Bill never shared that interest.

All my life I had the companionship of dogs. In my years at home my mother always had one around the place and when I was grown I also had some of my own. Bill complained about them on a regular basis and when we moved to the ranch, coerced me into giving up the Saint Bernards altogether. I never rehomed any but as each departed this world, it was not replaced. When we moved to the ranch we had only two remaining; one of those being Randy's pet. A few years before our move to the ranch, I had the best male Saint Bernard I would ever have and had shown him a few times quite successfully. He was a dream come true and the first dog I ever got pointed toward a championship. He was also the first dog I ever put a major win on and the excitement over that was thrilling. It was shortly after that big win that Bill began giving me a really hard time about showing and I gave in to his demands to quit. It would be almost 35 years later that I would finally show a dog to its championship for the first time. On one hand I felt if Bill disliked the dogs that much perhaps I should give him some time without them. On the other I felt his demands were unfair and motivated by his jealousy of anything that took my time and attention. He was seldom there during the day (and many nights and weekends) so he didn't see them much anyway: I was there all the time and I enjoyed having them around me.

Bill did not allow himself to care about animals. Maybe he was just too busy and too concerned about other things. He does tell the story of having to get rid of his one favorite dog when he was a child. I believe he was afraid to love one again. When the last St. Bernard died, it was not replaced with another dog of any breed. I was never happy about it but gave in to Bill's wishes as I did in so many areas throughout our marriage just to keep what little peace there was.

After a two-year period with no dog – and the only time in my life I was without one – I was permitted to get an Australian Cattle Dog (totally opposite of the size, looks, and hair coat that I preferred) as it was something closer to Bill's liking. To have a dog, period, I took advantage of the situation. We named her Kimberly and mostly called her Kimi. She was a wonderful dog and was a great help to me on the ranch with the cattle: I enjoyed her companionship for 14 years.

Kimberly was a credit to her breed when working cattle. She saved a cowboy from possible serious injury by using all her 25 pounds to back down an 1,800-pound bull that attacked him after throwing him in a rodeo. She went after cattle so fast she gained the nickname "The Canine Torpedo" with some of our rodeo friends. I truly adored her and learned to overlook the fact she was not a St. Bernard.

After Kimi died she was replaced by another Cattle Dog, Abby. Abby was less to my liking in looks even than Kimi and a pup I never would have chosen. Bill had picked her out while he was at a rodeo and I was in Canada. He gave her to me as a surprise. To avoid hurting his feeling, I never told him how I felt and just accepted her as from God's hands. I trusted she would grow on me so to speak. She was to teach me a lot about inward beauty – things I needed to be taught. There is a chapter about that in "Lessons From A Saint" as well. Abby was also a big help, and was actually a better cattle working dog than Kimi, although with a much different personality. She was with us for 10 years and was loved by all as well. As much as I enjoyed each of those dogs I still longed for a Saint Bernard. I asked Bill on a regular basis for permission to have one to no avail. I often thought of just going ahead and getting one without his approval, but I wanted to do things God's way and, truthfully, I didn't want to put up with the constant grief I would get from Bill if I did.

Each year at Christmas time I was hopeful Bill would give me a card, which would entitle me to search for that special Saint puppy. One year he did give me a gift he felt would make me happy. It was a ceramic Saint to sit on a shelf. It was beautiful and I cried, not because he got me such a beautiful gift, but because he didn't allow me to have the real thing. Looking at the artificial one made me painfully aware of how much I wanted a live one.

It was yet another year or more after giving me the ceramic Saint before Bill told me I could get a Saint puppy. My last Saint had been a wonderful, excellent quality show dog and I wanted another of good enough quality to show. After he gave me permission to buy a puppy it took me ten months to locate a show puppy to fit the description of what I wanted. I couldn't believe how hard it was but it was worth the wait.

Brooke came into our lives and brought us all the enjoyment I knew possible with a Saint. Everyone, including Bill, loved her. She was instrumental in the writing of my first book: "Lessons From A Saint" and she is the one on the front cover of that book. She was a delight and I suffered deeply when I lost her at the age of five due to repeated bouts with pneumonia. I missed her terribly for a very long time. She gave me one pup in her lifetime, a large and beautiful (inside and out) male who was our special boy, Shane. Bill thought Shane was the best dog and had a special love for him. He wouldn't dream of ever giving him up for any reason. We thoroughly enjoyed watching him grow and share our lives with us. Unfortunately Shane was to die at an early age as well, as he developed Addison's Disease and I was without a Saint once again.

Bill was getting more lenient about having dogs in the house and talked often about wanting a beagle to hunt with. Since moving to the ranch, we had no kennel whatsoever. My dogs were kept in the entry room and were yard trained so I had no problem letting them out when necessary. I did get Bill a beagle at one point, but we had no choice but to keep him on a chain. Both we, and the dog, were unhappy with that. Rather than keep him like that, I found a new home for him.

Beagles are such natural hunters they cannot be trusted out in the yard alone and are next to impossible to keep home unless penned. Because of that a beagle could not live with the other dogs in the house and just get turned out with them to relieve itself. He would be off and running in no time. I was opposed to having a beagle on a chain, in a small kennel, or worse yet one running the neighborhood and told Bill I would not take care of one under any of those conditions. Another problem was the hunting dogs were ignored most of the year and only used for a matter of weeks during hunting season. I didn't think that was fair to the dog.

While Bill understood that and basically agreed with my argument, he seemed to long so for a beagle that I thought I probably could fence in a large area of the yard for one. We have far more yard than we use and there is a section behind the house no one ever visited except me on the lawnmower. It would be perfect: I began to plan.

One given to love surprises, both as the initiator and the recipient, I was able to plan and pull off a wonderful surprise by driving Bill 300 miles, putting a beagle puppy in his arms, and then letting him know it was his 65th birthday present. He couldn't believe it; I was excited, but I had no idea where this would lead.

From the very moment Bonnie was placed in his arms, she and Bill were inseparable. Even on the way back home, *he* wanted to take care of her. He had never so much as fed one of my dogs and now he wanted to be the one to care for this three-pound joy giver. I was surprised and delighted.

One of the most astounding things I observed was the thoughtfulness developing in Bill. To this point he basically showed none to anyone. He had no hesitation of interrupting someone regardless of what they were doing. It didn't matter if it caused gross inconvenience or discomfort to them – he just didn't give it a thought. He would never remain in his chair even with a sleeping child in his lap if he wanted to get up: It never occurred to him to think of someone else's comforts. Now he didn't want to bother this tiny pup. To watch him contort his 180 pounds climbing out of a reposed reclining chair to avoid disturbing Bonnie instead of dumping her on the floor as he would have previously, was amusing and refreshing. Unbelievably, this beagle had taught him a lot about having and showing consideration for others. God uses the strangest things sometimes but He knows what will work.

Bill had a license plate on the front of his truck with a picture of a beagle and "his girl's" name on it. She went to work with him almost every day and often rode in the heavy equipment with him as well. She was well known at the local restaurant where she regularly received a complimentary piece of toast on her visits. At home she and Bill chased each other around the house and I heard his laughter ringing throughout the rooms. She transformed his life! He had never laughed so often nor had I ever seen him so tender.

Once Bill had a dog he could enjoy, the previous limits to areas of the house were abolished. Bonnie had the run of the house! It was truly enjoyable having a pup roaming the entire house and I loved to see her curled up with Bill each evening in his recliner. After getting pleasure from this association for a couple of months and watching him have so much fun with her, I told Bill we needed "his" and "hers" Beagles. I told him I was jealous and wanted one for my recliner. He agreed. I returned to the breeder I got his beloved pet from for another.

But since I enjoyed showing dogs so much, I got a show beagle pup for myself. What a joy she was and what fun she was to show. Talia earned her championship in the conformation show ring and was such a delight to be around. She was a perpetual puppy for most of her life and her antics kept us laughing. At the same time, she was very sweet and docile, winning everyone over with her engaging personality. Bonnie was a little more like me – couldn't sleep late, couldn't relax easily, always on the alert and always trying to take care of everything. It seems opposites truly do attract as Bill and I seemed to have acquired and fallen in love with these animals that were opposite our natural personalities.

After no dog was allowed even in our living room, it is still a wonder to me they soon shared our bed. Bill couldn't disappoint his girl by denying her his company for any reason. The very spring after I got Bonnie for Bill, through a tradeoff for riding lessons for our friend Gene's daughter, Gene fenced in close to an acre of our yard with chain link we had accumulated from job salvages. We installed doggie doors so the dogs can come and go from our entry room. The entry room has a large door to the outside to accommodate the Saint and another smaller door only the beagles can get through, giving them access to the main part of the house. When Shane (the Saint) is too dirty for the house, he can be contained in the entry room while the privileged ones get the run of the house. They are a little easier to clean and clean up after. They all have brought so much joy to our lives.

The only downside to the entire dog thing was the guilt I felt at times as I watched them totally take over our house. Every time my mother left for Texas and had to leave her dogs she left them with me, as I was the only animal lover in our family back east. I used to get angry having to put up with her chihuahua lying on the back of my couch looking out the window. Now I have beagles on the back of anything they want!

At dog shows I gravitated to the Saint Bernard ring and watched my favorite breed show. I met a lady who had top quality Saints who would let me sit and pet her dogs. It gave me my Saint "fix" I would say. In 2010 she asked me if I would like one of her dogs on a coownership until such time as I would get a championship title on her and pay for her with two puppies from future breeding's. I jumped at the chance. Cornerstone's Chasing Time (Hope) came home with me and filled a huge emotional need for me. She was about perfect. I did show her to her championship and beyond – getting a Grand Championship title on her. She is the perfect farm dog as well. God does give the best gifts.

In my earlier years, I desired such gifts believing God meant them to be tangible and enjoyable 'things'. I have since been taught a lot about true gifts, whether tangible or spiritual, that the Lord bestows on us and that generally those gifts are to be used to serve Him. He has blessed me in many such ways. While we all have spiritual gifts, our Father God wants to give us material gifts to enjoy as well. We must be trustworthy with those gifts and make sure they are never used to draw us away from the Giver. One such gift was Dani.

It was a January day and we were in our indoor arena. Lew Sterrett was there to help me out with a filly that needed handling and started under saddle. Lew is the originator of Sermon On The Mount – a message given while training an unbroken horse. Lew is one of the nations most noted and experienced horse trainers. At this time he was beginning to travel quite extensively to other states demonstrating the training practices he used. As he trains a horse, Lew draws parallels between the relationship of man and horse and man and God. Much horse training knowledge can be learned from observing these Sermons making them very interesting for horse owners and fanciers, but even more beneficial is the spiritual teaching that is sent forth at the same time. It is a tremendous outreach that affords countless opportunities to share the gospel of Christ and provide every day help for living the Christian life to its fullest.

"Bunny" was a three year old filly. Due to the time restraints I was under, I had let her run with two other fillies her age in a pasture attached to a barn they could run in and out of at will. They had been in that area together since they were weaned at four months of age. She was virtually untouched other than when we would trap the three of them in an area tight enough they couldn't move while they got necessary inoculations and deworming. She was as wild a horse as we ever had.

I had used Lew's methods on other horses with great success but he was often looking for horses to work with for teaching sessions to benefit others who would observe and learn by doing so. I asked him if he wanted to work with her as I knew she would be beyond ordinary. He said he did. I knew she was going to be difficult, and indeed she was. It was very tough getting her into a trailer to get her the 400 plus feet to the indoor arena.

We then herded her into the round pen we had set up at the far end of the arena where her training would take place.

Lew was in the habit of taking a horse that had no training and working it in the pen to teach it to listen to, focus on, and trust in, him. It is done gently, eliminating any fear the horse may have. With that done, he then would ride the animal. This was usually accomplished within an hour, often less.

Bunny was an exception. Lew went in the pen and began working with her. Three hours later he quit for the day. He had gotten no further than to be able to walk up to her and touch her. She would have to wait until tomorrow for the next session.

The next day he picked up where he left off and worked with her another three hours before he was able to saddle and ride her. To this day she remains the one who took the longest to train. His patient handling enabled her to become fit enough to travel extensively with him while he presented his sermons across the country, some of those sessions in large stadiums. She was so totally changed from that first day; exhibiting a sweet, willing disposition that made her a hit wherever she went as she demonstrated her trust in her master to the point he could lay her down in the midst of extreme noise and confusion and sit on her and speak to people. Bunny went on to be a top contender in rodeo barrel racing. She is an example of what God wants to and can do with us if we will place our trust in, focus on, and allow Him to do the teaching.

While I watched Lew work with Bunny in our home arena something I had been thinking of just days earlier was back in my mind. I had said to him, "You know if there was one thing I'd spend money on for myself, it would be a small, beautiful, palomino filly." Even as I thought about it I knew it would be extremely hard to find just what I was looking for.

I had had many palominos over the years – it wasn't just any palomino I wanted – she would have to be special. If I couldn't find just what I wanted, I'd continue to go without. It wasn't something I had to have, just something I'd like. I had no sooner said that when Lew replied, "You need to come with me to Georgia. I'm going to present some Sermons at one of the largest and best known palomino breeders in the country." My heart skipped a beat, I'm sure. Maybe there was a possibility of finding that special horse?

Lew was going to Singing Pines Plantation in March. He asked Bill and me to go along with him mainly so I could look at their horses. Upon arriving I found a small four-year-old filly covered in long, white, winter hair but I could picture what she must look like underneath and I liked what I saw. I asked the owners, Benham and Louise Stewart, how much they had to have for her and they informed me they couldn't sell her to me at that time. They were having a production sale the next month and she was already advertised as being offered in the sale. I couldn't get her out of my mind. She was exactly what I was looking for. They encouraged me to come back for the sale and buy her but getting away once in a year was a big feat for Bill and me. I couldn't conceive getting away twice in one year especially with the two trips only about six weeks apart.

God worked things out (and many things had to be worked out) and we did make that second trip. Bill, Lew, and I, along with two of our granddaughters, made the journey in our motor home. As soon as we got there I headed for the little mare I hoped to be able to purchase. I found her in a stall and hardly recognized her. They had done some extensive work on her coat and she was completely shed out to a shining golden palomino. She had a long flowing mane and tail and she was gorgeous! Feasting my eyes on her beauty, I was a bit depressed at the same time. I knew in my heart there was no way I could afford her.

We all pitched in and helped the Stewart's get the large number of horses to be sold ready for the ring. We girls got the bathing job. Dutifully we bathed one horse after another. Bittersweet was the time spent bathing this special horse I wanted. She was sweet and a pleasure to work around making me want her even more.

The day and time of the sale approached. From the first time I laid eyes on the mare I oscillated between hoping there was some way I could own her and fearing I never would. I prayed; others prayed with and for me, knowing of my desire. I also vacillated with being at ringside or not when she sold. I did not want to put myself through seeing her go to someone else. In the end I was there – mostly because I knew I had to show my faith in God for the outcome. I had a set amount of money I felt I could spend as we had a sizable income tax refund check due us. It wasn't here yet, but I expected it most any day. I also had a horse at home I could sell but that takes time.

The bidding on the mare began and for a time stayed within my reach. It narrowed down to Bill, bidding for me, and one other individual whom I never saw. It slowed down while still in our range and I thought she was going to be mine when Benham took the microphone and informed the crowd of the fact that they were "missing out on something special here". "This filly typifies what I've spent 35 years breeding to get", he said.

While he didn't say so, the only drawback to the mare is that she is not very tall. People wanting to show want tall horse – she is very short – perfect for my five-feet-two-inches. After Benham's speech the bidding by the other party began again. It got to my breakoff point and we did not have the high bid. With a heavy heart I told Bill we couldn't go any higher. He ignored me and bid two more times. I secretly was happy to have him do so but I was concerned about the financial end of it at the same time. I kept telling him "we'd better not go any higher." He did end up being the high bidder but we were $1200.00 over my limit! I reasoned I'd still be able to afford her in time, but I had no money at the present. I gave the clerk a check, afraid of what the next week would bring if the income tax check didn't come, yet at the same time optimistic that God would work it out. I felt He wanted me to have her.

That evening, at midnight, Bill and I went down to the barn and loaded Dances On Stars into the trailer we had taken along "just in case". She had never seen a trailer before but walked right on in the dark with no hesitation. I was further impressed with her. We pulled out and Bill, Lew, and the girls went to sleep while I drove the first leg of the trip home. While I was driving I was talking to the Lord about what had just happened and what was about to happen. I thanked Him so much for the beautiful, special gift He'd given me and then asked Him to provide the money to pay for her. I told no one about my conversation with God concerning this issue. We arrived home Sunday evening around 7:00 and I put my treasure in a stall, saw to her needs, and went in the house.

The next morning while doing chores an acquaintance stopped in. Laura Lee was riding one of my three-year old's in the round pen as she was just being started under saddle. This gentleman had tried to get me to sell this particular filly to him several times before but I had no interest in doing so previously. I had repeatedly turned him down and eventually he quit asking. Now here he was in the arena and he asked again. This time I gave him a price and told him it was contingent upon him taking her that very morning. He agreed, left, and came back within the hour with a trailer and cash. By 10:30 Monday morning I had all but $700.00 of the money I needed to pay for my new horse with this sale!

How I praised God then and still do for providing the 'best' gifts for His children. Dani, as we call her, is still a special delight these nineteen years later and is called the "Barbie Doll" of horses. She *is* special! She has served God for most of those 19 years by carrying the American flag during our rodeo opening event and humbly bowing to the crowd. I marvel at how God had it planned and worked out from the time I first mentioned to Lew my desire for a palomino

By the way, one of the first things I did with Dani after having her home was to give her back to my heavenly Father. He can take better care of her than I can.

It had been over 25 years since I had given up on having that black horse of mine being the stallion I was hoping for and I turned him over to the Lord. Many other stallions had come and gone through our ranch and at the moment, I had none. It was fine with me.

A friend I knew from rodeos called me to tell me about a nice black stallion she thought I should buy. This one would be for breeding only as he was unable to be ridden due to race related injuries and lameness, but he was well bred and carried the bloodlines I preferred to breed into my several mares. Even though he sounded good, I didn't want another stallion at the time and told the owner I wasn't interested. Gigi would tell me several times over the next few months that I needed to see and buy this horse.

As circumstances would have it I was going to be making the seven-hour trip to the place where he was kept with one of my students who was buying a horse from the same place. I promised Gigi I would at least look at him while I was there thinking that would be the end of it. I had no intention of buying him. We made the trip, went into the barn, and my mind was changed with just one look. What a magnificent horse he was! His breeding was exactly what I would look for had I been looking, his conformation was excellent, and he had an impressive race record himself, and was the son of a famous racehorse. His disposition was fantastic. He was eighteen years old when I acquired him and I was very pleased with him and his subsequent offspring. I used to stand next to him and wonder what it would have been like to ride him as a four-year old. That was as far as the 'wishing' went. It didn't matter; I just thought he must have been an awesome youngster.

One of the mares I bred to that stallion was a favorite black barrel-racing mare I had, (the same one Jamie was to ride for her father) then 23 years old. She conceived and gave me a beautiful black colt, which I almost sold soon after birth as I just didn't need any more horses. I couldn't keep up with what I had. I decided not to sell him at that time and, over the next one and one-half years, had several opportunities to sell the colt but held onto him as I felt he would be worth more money later. I would wait.

God works in mysterious ways His wonders to perform. I was in the arena one day riding the then three-year old stallion and something was happening. For the first time in many years, I was looking forward to going to the barn and riding. I had lost much of the desire to do so by having to go to the barn daily whether I wanted to or not just to ride the horses I had in for training. I had done that for many years and it was becoming just so much work I was still training but I did it out of a sense of duty, nothing more. Now things were changing. This colt was so easy to train – so quick to learn. He was growing into a beautiful horse with a willing, gentle disposition. He was fun! I thanked God for him and my renewed pleasures.

One day I took a good look at him and realized what I had. I had a coal black stallion with desirable conformation for a breeding animal, along with the bloodlines, disposition and athletic abilities to justify that position in life for him! I didn't need it, didn't ask for it, and I had all but forgotten that desire that was so strong in my life for so many years, and now God, in His perfect timing, gave me what I had wanted so desperately over forty-six years before. Why did He do that? Because at that point He knew he could trust me with him: because now, this horse doesn't belong to me – he belongs to my Lord. He is His, to do with as He will. I'm crazy about this horse, but I hold him lightly as he is not mine. I will enjoy him as long as the Lord allows me to do so, but my primary focus must remain on my Lord and His plan for my life. I must remain trustworthy of this 'desire' fulfilled.

God had to wait on me to get my priorities straight, which resulted in changing the way I looked at the desires of my heart. I didn't even know what they really were, but He did. I was finally beginning to understand that He made my heart and He knew what would satisfy me. I thought I did, but I was way off base. He knew that above everything else, I wanted to serve Him and share Him and His goodness with others. That is my primary focus. These material gifts are just icing on the cake!

Chapter Thirty-Four

MORE EMOTIONAL TURMOIL

> *Philippians 4:6: "Be anxious for nothing, but in everything by prayer and supplication, with thanksgiving, let your requests be made known to God." (NKJV)*

It began almost immediately in May of 1976 with us taking over the deeply distressed company, all things instantly becoming my responsibility, and ultimately my fault when anything went wrong. I got extremely anxious and fearful about failing, knowing that it would all be blamed on me. I was too insecure to bear such responsibility as I had not yet learned to trust God for any of it. I tried to handle it all alone.

Shortly after acquiring sole responsibility for the business, we secured the beach replenishment project for Presque Isle. That we got the project was a miracle in itself, as it required a million-dollar bond from our insurance company to be considered. It was unthinkable with the financial condition we were in but nothing is ever done if you do not try and nothing is impossible with God so we applied for it. Miraculously and only because of God, we got the bond!

We had done this same project a number of times before and knew well how to do it. This particular time we ran into union problems though as the local union wanted our non-union company to use their union members to run our equipment. Bill himself and/or one of our regular full-time employees ran most of it. If the union had their way, Bill would not be able to run his own equipment and our people would have to sit on the sidelines. We could not afford to hire others for the wage they insisted on us paying while Bill and our employees did nothing.

Inasmuch as we chose not to do what they requested, they instigated trouble for us. Threats were made against employees and truckers. The State Police came to *my* home to warn *me* to stop allowing *our* truckers to cause problems and accused us of encouraging them to carry guns. None of their allegations were true. The other parties were guilty of those very things, but we were the ones assumed wrong. My fears increased.

In my regular devotions during this time, I was reading about the Israelites wandering in the desert for forty years due to lack of faith and trust in the Lord. I was fearful of that happening in my life and told the Lord if he would help me, I would trust Him. I reminded myself of the need of that commitment numerous times over the next many years as I was tempted to give up. I had little idea of just how much I did trust Him at that point in my life. I was to find out over the coming months and years.

The gravel pit we purchased just before the partnership dissolution was set up to be paid for by making one large yearly payment for five years. We had managed to do so each year until, as the last payment date approached, we had no funds. Always fearing the worst I knew then this would be the end of it all for us as we would lose the pit and our biggest source of income. I was so fearful and convinced of impending doom that each time a crisis arose, I immediately *knew* it was the end of the business and would have horrible ramifications for us personally.

Bill's discernment came into play once again when he suspected some things were not quite right with our insurance agent. We even mentioned that idea to our banker at a meeting as we were trying to borrow money to make that final payment on the pit. Our banker, a Christian man we admired, promptly, and with a patronizing attitude, told us that what we were alleging could not be possible as our agent was also a member of the board of directors of that particular bank and a highly respected man. It made me wonder what he thought of us. He nicely assured us that if there were a problem, it would have been due to our error. Once again, I felt like an idiot, totally incompetent, and inept. We dropped the subject. We did not get the loan.

It wasn't long after this meeting we received word our insurance agent had contracted a rare disease. He died within a matter of weeks thereafter. Soon after his death and just days before the deadline for our payment, we got a check in the mail from the attorney handling his estate. The check was for the exact amount due for that final payment: $20,000.00! There was a short explanation with the check stating some improprieties had been discovered in our agent's handling of our account and that for the past few years we had been overcharged the amount reflected by the reimbursement. Incredible is the only way to describe this entire situation.

Another time in the spring a problem concerning the gravel pit arose with the Department Of Environmental Protection and we were notified with this confusing and seemingly threatening letter. The letter came the day before Easter. I cannot recall the issue anymore; I only know I was sure we were in deep trouble with no way out. Again, I was terrified to the point of being emotionally paralyzed.

Easter morning, as was my habit, I went to the community sunrise service and left Bill at our church for the breakfast following. After that would be Sunday school and worship service. Normally, I would come home and do the chores (I do not "do" breakfast) then go back to church to join him. This particular day the weight of the problem I would have to face on Monday loomed so large in my mind that after chores, I could not return to church. I remained at home, immobilized with fear, unable to function at all.

Part of the reason for my slavery to this paralyzing fear became evident to me as I begged God for answers. He helped me realize much of my unrest was due to my still trying to hold onto things I thought I had let go of. I simply had not learned to trust Him to take care of me if the worst should happen.

I had always looked at my mother with a bit of disappointment due to her emotional weakness and her reliance on what we called in those days, nerve pills. I do not know what she took; I only knew she needed them. I felt that practice showed no faith in God at all. Now here I was lying on the couch so terrified about the future I would have taken a handful of them if I had to them. I did not, thank God, and so I had to find another way to deal with this gripping fear. I prayed and prayed, mostly for God to change my circumstances so I would have no need to fear. I felt Him directing me to his Word. I opened my Bible and looked up some of His wonderful promises and read them over and over for the next couple of hours. By focusing on them instead of the problem, this, too, He brought me through.

His word is full of such hope and encouragement. All that is needed to face anything life might throw at us is right at our fingertips. I read the verses repeatedly until I felt peace. It became a practice for me to use this method of dealing with the crippling fears I faced. Over the next months and years I spent many days going back to my Bible on an hourly basis to get enough help to get through the next hour.

That experience made me aware of the reality of the phrase: "There, but for the grace of God, go I". I know I am no better than those crippled by addictions of one kind or another, as without God's help, I am sure I would be just the same. I had no right to cast stones at mother when I suffered not only emotionally but also physically from the constant worry. Sometimes I wonder whether it is genetic, as my aunt and uncle had to depend on drugs to calm their nerves and fears. Doctors who were looking for ulcers, cancer, and other maladies due to the physical pain I felt were often checking me. For many years I was to suffer with spastic colon, a horribly painful inflammation of the bowel brought on by anxiety and worry. I endured many invasive procedures in doctor's efforts to find the cause. No physical reason was ever found – it always came back to my emotional state. Of course I denied any possibility that could be the truth. To admit that, even to myself, would be a significant sign of weakness.

Fear and worry together were my constant companions and always my first extreme emotions to any adverse situation. I'd heard people glibly make the remark, "Why pray when you can worry?" Unfortunately, while I did pray, I did not let go of the worry.

The horses that had always been my joy and release from pressure, even for short periods, were beginning to become problematic. There was little time to spend with them with everything else that was going on and now the little time I did spend with them was often problematic. When things were bad in the business, Bill looked to me to solve all the problems. If they were not solved, he resented any time I spent away from business matters. It could be evenings or weekends and well after business hours but he repeatedly told me I had no business spending time with the animals when I should be taking care of business.

Before the time of computers, cell phones, and the like that now help so much with the office work, I had to have a phone jack attached to a pole next to the outdoor arena so I could take a phone out there with me in order to do any training or to ride at all. I would ride, trying to get something accomplished with the horse I was on, but repeatedly I would have to stop what I was doing to answer the phone and then often drop everything to go take care of business. In the early days, we had no way of communicating between parties on the road or at the gravel pits and I was interrupted time and again sometimes to drive 20 miles or more one way just to give a message to Bill or deliver a piece of paper we so easily fax (or take a picture of and text) now. We put bells outside for the phone and a speaker for our two-way radio system to alert me to a phone ringing or a radio call so I could do some gardening or mow the lawn.

Because of the conflict over the horses, I began to question God about the matter. I asked Him if I should give up having the horses altogether and just concentrate on the business. Even in asking, I had a couple of problems with that: I was already burning myself out with the business and its problems and the horses were still my only relief from those pressures, although that relief was tempered by the fact that when I did spend time with them, I felt guilty about doing so. I knew I would be bitter should I give them up as I never felt it was God's will to do so, but Bill's will. At times, I came very close to doing so though, as I could not take Bill's constant badgering about it. I prayed and I hung on.

After agonizing about it for years, I came to the realization that God is the One who gave me the love for, and the talent with, animals that I have and that He must have done that for a purpose. I asked Him to allow me to use the horses for His honor and glory. Of course, what I had in mind at the time was achieving great fame and then being a witness for Him. He did allow me to keep them and He did use them for His glory but He did it His way and in His timing.

After breeding horses for several years, the herd had grown in size and we had a group of horses with much potential and value. All were good quality animals and it was difficult to part with any while they were too young to properly evaluate. They would be worth more when they were trained for barrels or roping and I also did not want to let that special one get away.

Even though I would make money on these horses Bill was not content to have me spend time with them and the guilt increased. Many times, in anger, he told me to get rid of them. After hearing it so many times, I decided to call his bluff and sell some. The very first time I sold one he got angry because I did! When I told him I did it because he told me to, he turned right around and told me he never said anything about getting rid of any horses. At times his behavior made me think I was losing my mind.

The guilt over me spending time anywhere but in the office became so great and so real, that even after several years of having things up to date and well covered with my office staff and the availability of cell phones and computers, I still had a hard time enjoying myself in the barn or anywhere away from the office. Guilt tried to rear its ugly head and tell me I should be in the office trying to do something.

Chpater Thirty-Five

THE HOME OFFICE

---

1 Corinthians 10:13: "No temptation has overtaken you except such as is common to man; but God is faithful, who will not allow you to be tempted beyond what you are able, but with the temptation will also make the way of escape, that you may be able to bear it." (NKJV)

It took me far too many years to even begin to do things for my Lord instead of always trying to please myself. I resented just about everything that didn't bring me pleasure or make my circumstances easier.

When we lived in the trailer, I traveled each day to the office in the old building at the gravel pit to take care of the business. It was very difficult leaving every day. Laura Lee was ten years old the first summer and I didn't like her alone at home. I would find friends to stay with her whenever possible but I still didn't like not being with her. I took her with me most often. It also made it difficult to leave home due to all the animals that needed watching. I hated leaving but I had no choice. I spent as few hours a day as possible in that office and did whatever of the work I could back in the trailer.

After spending two years in the trailer, the house was built and we moved in the summer of 1978. The house provided us with a full basement, although it was not finished – just a basement. There would have been plenty of room down there for an office but I wouldn't consider it. The problem was I could not stand being inside, period, let alone in a dark basement. When I designed the house, I did so making the entire south end of the living area all windows. Through those windows I could see the barn and close by enclosures and I could watch the animals in them. During the times I was stuck inside, I could at least see out. In the basement I would not have seen anything outside as it only has two small well windows below ground.

Upstairs in the house I had a large closet built on the end wall of the living room opposite those large windows. It was built to use for an office where I could close the doors and hide evidence of it away from the rest of the world. From there I would have a full view across the room and through those windows. With this space available, I brought the bookkeeping home. It helped. When we sold the building at the gravel pit a few years later, we lost the office space previously available anyway. But bringing the office home definitely turned out to be bittersweet.

I started the office in that closet in the living room. It worked okay until things progressed and it became far too small for working and storing all the business records. The business grew as well until it became impossible for me to handle everything by myself. Up to this point I did all the bookkeeping, payroll, invoicing, payments, telephone answering, radio dispatching, and handled all matters concerning insurance, legal and financial issues. On top of that there were the farm issues. The children were beginning to be of considerable help with chores but it was mostly me tearing down and trying to fix old fences, etc. I decided I needed some help for the office.

I didn't have too much trouble finding help. I began with one girl who worked with me until she moved out of town, and then I replaced her with another. Often, since they shared my home, I hired friends with no experience in our line of work, which made more work for me in training them or being constantly available for all the inevitable questions and situations only I could deal with. Another problem was I had no office other than my living room in which for her to work. I brought her into my home and shared my house with her five days a week for several years.

Things continued to grow until we absolutely did not have enough room for things in that closet. At that point the decision was made to remodel the basement to make more office space. There was already one finished room as it had been Randy's bedroom, now vacated as he had married and moved out. We started there, however for some time they still had to come upstairs to use one of our bathrooms. When the remodeling was completed, we had a total of four offices in our basement plus a bathroom so they didn't have to come upstairs to use the facilities any longer. For the next 15 years these rooms would serve as the offices for up to four employees at a time.

There is no outside entrance to the basement thus all business traffic had to come into the house. The girls traveled through to get to their offices; prospective employees filling out job applications sat in my entry room while they did so. All deliveries and sales people came to my door. It made it almost impossible to keep my dogs away from visitors as they were housed in that entry room. Bill didn't allow dogs in the house at the time with the exception of the kitchen and dining room and then only when they were clean which in this climate was not often. They barked and carried on every time someone approached the house and it was quite annoying for all. The employees weren't dog trainers and it made it very difficult for them trying to calm the dogs while also trying to handle the business situation at hand. The presence of so much activity and so many people in and out of our home made every day a nightmare while I tried to grieve over my losses and deal with al the pressures of life and business.

Trying to stay separated from some of the business issues was almost impossible for me as I had to watch the dogs each time someone came to the house. I could not be upstairs doing work in my house as people would come and interrupt me. Due to that situation I was constantly frustrated, as I cannot stand my house less than neat and tidy but finding time to keep it that way was impossible. If I was downstairs in my office and someone came, I would have to drop what I was working on and go mind the dogs for however long it took. The phone rang from 5:30 AM until 10:00 PM or later and it was mostly business related. After many, many years of these constant interruptions I made the decision that we should allow the answering machine to record calls for us during dinner so we could at least have some peace. I can remember how hard Bill fought me over the issue. We had never considered such a drastic measure and it was a difficult new pattern to develop, but one much needed. Prior to that decision, we never considered not being interrupted – it was a way of life – our way of life. We knew no other.

As people approached the main entry door, they would pass by our patio doors, which open into the dining room. Through those doors they could see the dining room, kitchen, and living room. If they were to see me there, they wanted to talk to me. If I closed them off with shades, I lost the beauty for which they were intended in the first place. I felt guilty hiding even when it was possible but for sanity reasons (mine) learned to do so often until the visitor was gone.

Between the lack of visual privacy, the endless needs of the office employees for my attention, the phone calls, the constant attending to the dogs, and people in and out of my house at least five days a week, sometimes more, I had virtually no privacy – ever! It was extremely difficult for me, being a loner by nature. I never had time to myself and I was not dealing with it well emotionally. The house I had longed for and now had lived in for over 23 years was still only a house. It was not mine: even though I was raising a family in it at the same time, it was not a home. It all belonged to the business. So did I.

After 14 years of living like this an idea came to me to put a small house trailer out by the road next to the big garage some 400 feet from the house and put the offices out there. As I voiced that idea to others, there was some concern about moving out at all. The office employees were all so dependent upon me we all wondered how we would be able to handle being that far apart. There were questions and issues that needed my input on a constant basis. If I was upstairs, they came and found me. If I was outside working or riding, they tracked me down. I was needed for just about every decision. But with the new phone capabilities including intercom features, we were hopeful it would work out and decided it would be worth a try.

Bill agreed to the plan and didn't take long to get a trailer and bring it home, but he let other things come first before taking the time to make it useable for us and the project was put on the back burner. While I got the trailer, I watched it sitting in the driveway for months with nothing being done to it or about it. It was to be close to another year before we were able to move the offices into it. I struggled with depression on a constant basis, but this ordeal was causing me to slip even further into that pit. I was aware of it but I did not care, as I was losing my will to fight.

The transition to the trailer was made in 2001. It had myriad problems and issues but the inconveniences were well worth it. It would take another ten years before my house began to feel like a home.

Chapter Thirty-Six

DEPRESSION AND THE CONVERSATION

Psalm 86:1: "Bow down Your ear, O Lord, hear me; For I am poor and needy." (NKJV)

Bill and I were on a short vacation in the late winter of 2000 and we had our cattle dog Abby with us. I was depressed with all the business, financial, and other problems, but this depression seemed more than even that, which was enough. It had lasted for over a year to the point that I didn't care much about anything. For the first time in my life I could sleep in the morning after the sun was up. The activities that used to bring me pleasure no longer interested me. I was half-heartedly asking the Lord to show me what was wrong so I could deal with it as I didn't seem able to find the underlying cause of my hopeless feelings.

At a truck stop along the way, I took the time to take Abby out for a walk to do her business. I was asking the Lord again, "What is the reason for the way I feel?" This time I felt the answer. My thoughts gravitated to the things I'd been struggling with, along with my attached emotions, and I began to see I had just bottled them up inside me and sealed them tightly with a cap of hopelessness. I thought about the deaths and separations that were so hard on me, the loss of money and dignity through the business problems, the loss of a meaningful relationship with my in-laws due to misunderstandings, the loss of any time for or to myself, the loss of privacy in my house (still not a home due to being open for business – the trailer sitting unusable in the driveway). I even felt the loss of the desire unfulfilled of having a Saint Bernard to show and be my companion as Bill at this point in time had refused to allow me to get another.

As I listened to the Lord, I began to comprehend I had not dealt with the losses as I should have and I began to realize they were a big part of my despondent spirit.

Knowing was the beginning but I either didn't know what to do about it or wasn't ready to do anything about it and things proceeded along the same gloomy path for the next few months. I was thinking about it but that was about it. Reluctant to change myself, I just wanted circumstances to change for the better; then I would feel better I was sure.

Our son, Randy, and his family, live across the road from us down in the woods. It was a Sunday afternoon and we were having a cookout over there as we often do in nice weather. We were out of butter and needed more so I offered to go back over to our house and get some. I drove over and got the butter and was headed back when I felt an overwhelming need to be alone.

I parked next to the pond, got out of the truck, and sat along the edge of the water in the warm summer sunshine. How good it felt to be there alone with my thoughts. I had no desire to even move. After sitting there for a few minutes the phone began ringing in the big garage about 50 feet from where I was sitting and I knew the family was looking for me. Normally I would have gotten up and gone back over to make everyone happy but this time I didn't care. I couldn't move; I sat there.

I so needed the Lord in this situation. I felt the time was now. I started thinking and then saying out loud: "Lord, You say You are always with us and that You want to be my best friend and help me in every need." I looked over to my right side and pictured Him sitting beside me there on the grass. I continued: "So, I know You are sitting right here next to me and I'm happy to have You here. You know what is going on; I believe You have shown me most of my problems. Now I need to know what to do about them. What are we going to do from here?"

It felt like He was sitting right next to me and it was so natural to converse with Him as I would have another friend. What a blessed experience. Jesus became very real to me that day. I don't remember exactly what He said but I felt His presence and love in a new way. I also felt His assurance that He would, indeed, take care of me if I would trust Him. While I had a long, hard road ahead of me, it was the beginning of my healing.

Chapter Thirty-Seven

BUILDING WITH A BETTER PURPOSE

Colossians 3:23: "And whatever you do, do it heartily, as to the Lord and not to men." (NKJV)

Building the physical components of the ranch was one thing, but God was beginning to build other things as well. For one, the rodeo itself was not the only thing God accomplished by us holding it. I believe the year was 2000 and a new undertaking was about to emerge. It was certainly not anything I looked for or expected.

I received a phone call from a stranger one-day inquiring about an upcoming clinic to be held at our facility by Lew Sterrett. Due to the event being held here, our phone number was listed as a contact number for those desiring more information about the occasion. The woman who called was primarily seeking direction to the ranch.

In an effort to explain the easiest and quickest way to find us, I asked her if she had ever been to the rodeo. After 16 years the rodeo was pretty well known in the area and most people can relate to us quickly through it. I was surprised to hear her tell me she had never heard of it. I asked her where she lived; she replied "Union City". Shocked even more, I asked her how long and she said for quite a number of years. She began asking me about the rodeo and our facility.

We talked for some time and during the conversation, it became apparent we were both Christians and began talking about things other than the rodeo. She told me she and a friend had begun a Christian camp for underprivileged children just two years earlier. Starting out with a small number of children, they camped for a weekend that first year in the back yard of one of the parents. It was such a success that by the next year so many more kids wanted to come it was apparent it would not work with such limited facilities. They were now looking into finding a place they could afford to rent as the camp was growing much faster than they had expected.

The places they had contacted were quite expensive and the camp had no money. They do not charge kids to come to camp as their parents cannot afford to send them. For many of the children this is the only way they would ever be able to attend a camp. Everything done with and for the camp was done through donations, from the grounds to the food for the kids. They asked me if I knew of any place they might look into.

Our conversation led me to tell her to give me time to talk to my husband and then to her and her partner. Bill and I agreed we should meet with them. I had always said I wanted to use the place for the glory of God and this looked like an opportunity to do just that. We set up a meeting, the two women in charge of the camp came out, and I met with them in our clubhouse at the arena.

As they arrived they became extremely excited about what they saw – lots of wide-open space and a big indoor facility. Entering the clubhouse created more excitement as they discovered a kitchen and two restrooms complete with a shower in each. They admitted being apprehensive about our willingness to allow them access to the facility or, should we be willing to let them use it, being able to afford it.

We talked: they explained their needs. At this time they were only in need of a facility for one week. As they told us of the counselors, nurse, and other helpers that would be staying it sounded quite well planned. We saw no reason not to allow them the use of the property for a week. Again, concerned about cost, they were most relieved when we informed them we wanted no money from them. It was our service to the Lord.

The coordinator, Barbie Yoder did, indeed, do a great job of organizing the camp. Campers have a full day of supervised activities, including several Bible studies and time set aside for such things as crafts, swimming, and other activities. One of the holding areas of the arena was the designated Chapel and services were held each evening.

What began with two families in a back yard seven years ago became a four to five weeklong camping schedule, a different group coming each week. Some weeks they had up to 70 or more children at a time.

After several years of sleeping in tents and putting up with water running in and through their "beds" during heavy storms other possibilities for bunking were explored. Through Carpenters for Christ and other means, five bunkhouses were built along with two more cabins providing office space and sleeping quarters for office personnel. Each year something else was done to improve the situation for both campers and directors.

As the campers were told the story of Jesus, many new Christians were baptized in our pond. This was an exciting event to witness. Only God knows the far reaching effects of such an outreach. How privileged we were to be a part of it.

As a young person, of all equine events, I enjoyed jumping the most. The opportunity to pursue that discipline ended soon after marriage and the kids arrived as the whole family got hooked on rodeo. I had to find another event in which to compete. My only other choice was barrel racing. That was okay as I liked the fast pace. Being a perfectionist and horse trainer, I quickly learned the right and wrong way to perform the sport, inasmuch as I was doing it all wrong and looked like a fool among those who were doing it right!

For too many years the ranch was quite an expense as the herd accumulated and nothing was sold. Selling the horses off helped considerably but current expenses had to be met and we needed to find an answer for accomplishing that. With the indoor arena and addition making it possible, we began holding barrel racing, roping, and team penning events to generate some income and offset the expenses of the horse ranch.

The ranch has grown into a business in and of itself. It is a lot of hard work and is frustrating beyond belief at times trying to make contestants and the public happy, but it does pay the bills and gives people a place to come and compete and just have a good time regardless of weather.

The knowledge I gained from other professionals and the experience I had with training and barrel racing led me to another venture. Because I am a perfectionist and horse trainer, it was difficult for me to ignore some of the tactics used by competitors while running their horses in this demanding sport.

Barrel racing requires a lot of mental stability on the part of the horse to handle the demands placed upon it. This demand is in the hands of the rider. If the rider is only trying to get himself around the course as quickly as possible without thought of how he handles the horse, it can cause the horse some real discomfort as well as slower times. This, then, can lead to all sorts of problems, as many horses will not be anxious to do something that causes them pain. Some riders then get more frustrated and often take it out on the horse; some try to "muscle" them through the course thinking they are just being stubborn or willful, this leading to yet more problems. Beyond the ill treatment to the horse, those undesired actions can lead to danger to the rider as a horse may rebel by rearing, bucking, or running off.

My love for horses could not bear the sometimes downright inhumane way the animals were being handled. Having learned the right way the hard way (and with help from professionals) and competing for many years successfully, I was happy to receive a request to give a talk on the proper way to train a barrel horse. That was quite successful and I quickly progressed from just talking about it to demonstrating proper techniques.

This episode then led to a career of doing clinics, giving lessons, doing demonstrations, and even holding annual barrel camps. Barrel camp is a five-day training clinic wherein the students, along with their horses, stay at the ranch for the period, students riding and receiving instruction for most hours of the day. It is most rewarding to see the number of competitors learning to handle their horses in a manner that allows them to do what they are asking them to do properly and to work as a team to do it safely.

In addition to the horse/handler training, with God's help, I'm working on building confidence and character in the students that come to me and am always ready to share the love of Christ with them. Those opportunities are what this business is all about.

God definitely had a reason for having me keep the horses.

Chapter Thirty-Eight

PHYSICAL ATTACKS AND LIFE CHANGES

Psalm 46:1: "God is our refuge and strength, a very present help in trouble. Therefore we will not fear." (NKJV)

Both Bill and I had various physical issues and surgeries we had to deal with over the years. Each of us had knee surgeries, Bill hernia surgery. My surgeries started with the birth of my daughter and subsequent blood clots, requiring major surgery, and an appendectomy and a tubal ligation, just months later. The reason for the appendectomy was to help avoid the need for future surgeries as the doctor informed me that any surgery would carry a serious risk of death from blood clots. I had a hysterectomy at age 24, (they left my ovaries) several nose surgeries, bladder surgery, etc., but the physical issues seemed to escalate when we hit the year 2000. That was the year a mass was discovered on one of my ovaries during a routine examination. The word scared me to death. I only associated it with cancer and I was sure that was what I had. The biopsy report would take several days to return and until then I could do nothing but wait and pray. I used that weekend of beautiful weather to spend time with Bill out on the pond in the paddle boat just floating and enjoying the beauty of the surroundings. I fully expected to get bad news and wanted to soak up as much of the goodness of my life as I could for the days ahead. The report, however, indicated the mass was benign, and after it was removed, (I had bladder surgery at the same time) I was as good as new. I was constantly grateful for God's hand of protection on us both through these episodes.

A few years after that, I had my first blood clotting episode since 1966 when Laura Lee was born. The clots (always plural) were discovered in time and didn't move past the calf of my leg thus it didn't keep me down at all. It was a bit unnerving, though, to have had this problem for the second time.

Somewhere in the neighborhood of 2008 a horse stepped on the outside of one of my feet and broke the bone. I was bringing her into the barn while starting evening chores when something spooked her and she jumped right on it. The timing of that accident was fortunate in that it happened the night before I was scheduled for a pre-op exam for bunion surgery to be performed the day after. I had the foot checked out during that visit which confirmed the break and thus had it repaired when the bunion surgery took place saving an additional operation. Not too long after that surgery, it was discovered the screws used for repairing the break were not staying in place and I had to have them surgically removed. A year later I had the first bunion surgery repeated and a similar operation of the opposite foot. By now I'd had so many surgeries I had forgotten the warning given my by the doctor who had saved my life in 1966. This doctor was one of the most noted vascular surgeons in the US and certainly knew what he was talking about. With his warning that any and all surgeries should be avoided - as each carried a real possibility of causing life-threatening blood clots - I should have realized by that time just the way God was holding onto me. I didn't though, and took His grace through it all for granted. At this point, my surgery total was up to fourteen.

Bill had both rotator cuffs repaired during the years in and around these other events.

In 2002, Bill began having noticeable problems with his memory and things began to fall apart in many areas.

In the spring of 2009, Bill had a stomach upset with symptoms similar to something that seemed to be going around at the time so when he complained about it hurting him, at first I didn't pay too much attention. When it didn't seem to improve after a couple of weeks, I took him to the doctor and tests revealed there was cancer in one of his kidneys. Fortunately it was completely encapsulated and contained to that area. He had surgery to remove the kidney a few weeks later and recovered from it well, never needing follow up treatment.

I had a torn rotator cuff and was unable to practice team roping as I would like, so I made arrangements to have it fixed. As always, with elective surgery, I chose a winter month to avoid losing working time during good weather. In January of 2010 I had the surgery. Due to my former history of blood clots, a filter was placed in my body to prevent clots that might form due to surgery from traveling to my heart and lungs. That assured me I had nothing to worry about. Two weeks to the day after the surgery I had a pain in my lower left back that was unlike any I'd had before. Since it was unfamiliar to me, I assumed it must be a kidney stone as they say that pain is pretty severe. Because I thought it was a stone, I didn't hurry to the hospital as I believed they would just send me back home to pass it. I waited three days from the initial pain to go get it checked out still expected it to be "nothing". Shortly after entering the hospital and having a cat scan, I was shocked to learn that I had two blood clots in one lung, one in the other, one in my shoulder, and several in the calves of both legs! I spent ten days in the hospital – a hospital that was within sight of the building where the Erie Kennel Club dog show was held (which I always looked forward to showing at) and I was there, in that hospital, during the days of the show. That was disappointing. There was no choice but to put me on a blood thinner that I would take for the rest of my life, and that would be the beginning of a tremendous life change for me.

I believe I had taken God's care of me a bit lightly prior to this, but what He brought me through this time opened my eyes to the extraordinary way He was preserving my life! Only by His grace did I survive any of the now three blood clotting episodes, that I did is nothing short of proof of the miracles He performed for me. This was glaringly evident when I was told those blood clots that were in my lungs had to have traveled from my shoulder *through* my heart to get there! One cannot be safer anywhere than in His care.

I had spent the majority of my life training horses, barrel racing, and roping. Not only was it what I loved doing, it also provided much-needed income on the ranch. Leaving the hospital on blood thinner required some serious thinking and choice-making. I felt the same – no one would know anything was different; my abilities were the same. The problem was that any serious accident with a horse - be it falling on me, or bumping into me and slamming me against a wall; anything that caused a blow of any kind could initiate an internal bleed. I may not even recognize it at first until it was too late to do anything about it. I was informed that, should I have such a bleed, I would have about 45 minutes to be in intensive care. That would be impossible where I live. My personal concerns aside, I knew Bill needed me. So, I made the agonizing decision to quit training horses and to stop barrel racing and roping. It was a heart-breaking decision.

That decision didn't come easily nor was it made quickly. After the shoulder healed, I went back to training my black horse on barrels in anticipation of starting to compete on him. A few months after recuperating from the surgery, I was riding alone in the arena on a Friday afternoon. As I was working San on running the barrel pattern, I felt God speaking to me about it all. As I ran him toward a barrel and made a fast turn, I could "hear" God say, "What if he had fallen on you? You are out here alone and you could be in serious trouble." I ignored Him at first and continued to work and run, but I was beginning to hear these same words with each run, each barrel; each turn. Any horse can fall at any time, without warning. I felt I finally got the message and told my Lord, "Okay. I'll quit barrel racing as I like team roping so much better anyway." I felt I could live with that.

The next day we were holding a team roping competition at our place and I told the secretaries at the desk that when a certain man came to sign up, remind him he owed me $20 from the previous roping. They immediately came back with, "Oh, he won't be here today. He just got out of intensive care yesterday after his horse fell on him while roping a steer. He almost died!" Immediately I felt the Lord telling me I was to give this up as well. That was much harder to do – much more difficult than giving up the barrel racing. I still teach barrel racing and don't have too hard a time giving up the training, but I still do not like to watch team roping as I miss it so much.

Three years after the last clotting episode, I broke my back and two discs herniated while trying to lift a hay elevator up onto the hitch of a tractor so that I could put it away for the winter. I'm still struggling with the effects of those injuries.

In 2006 Bill was officially diagnosed with Alzheimer's disease *and* dementia. He was put on medication immediately and monitored with regular visits to a neurologist. Along with the loss of my dream job with horses, I was about to lose much more.

Chapter Thirty-Nine

NEW DIRECTION

Job 1:21:b "The Lord gave, and the Lord hath taken away; blessed be the name of the Lord." (NKJV)

In my studies of the Bible and in the other material I read and heard many other places, I was led to believe, "If the Lord takes something away from you, He will replace it with something better." I watched my life, in a sense, from that moment on to see if it actually was true. I have seen it proven correct in many circumstances. I believe it *is* true.

As a newly committed Christian (really trying to commit, not just look for handouts from God) I struggled with surrendering my animals to him. I never got over the thought that should I do that, He would, indeed, immediately take them! I was still not prepared to give them up.

I had spent the better part of my life with horses and had had innumerable pleasures and satisfactions with and from them. I had achieved significant accomplishments in both barrel racing and team roping in and out of the rodeo arena and was a noted clinician with a good and widespread reputation for my abilities with horses and working with people. I never looked far enough ahead to think it would ever change. It was my life. For the biggest part of my life it was where I got the little self-esteem I had. To think of ever giving this part of my life up was to think about my life pretty much being over.

After the last bout with blood clots – this one every bit as life threatening, if not more, than the first time, I was put on an anticoagulant and told I would have to stay on it for the rest of my life. I likely would have taken the chance and gone on and lived my life as I had been even so. After all, I think with all my years of riding, I had only been actually bucked off about six times. I wasn't worried about that. I have had horses fall on me though, but in each one of those cases it was never anything very serious. Still, I had to consider that, as told earlier in this book, I was not close enough to medical help to be assured of timely lifesaving aid should it be needed: I was confident I would be okay. But you never know for sure.

I now had Bill to deal with and it was unimaginable to me what would happen to him if something happened to me first, and thus I made the heart-wrenching decision to give up my dream and put him and his needs first. It was a very difficult resolution to make and took immense self-control to live by it and keep a healthy attitude. I still got on the occasional horse to do some slow work and bring home a point I was trying to make to a student, but that was the most I felt I should do. When, only a few years later, I fractured my back and two discs herniated it gave me far more reason to stay off the horses. I still yearn to get on and fix one, more often than anyone knows, but along with realizing no horse is worth me getting hurt or killed (or worse live with a stroke from a brain bleed or some similar malady) I feel the Lord has told me that part of my life and dream is over.

God led me into another dream I'd had for just as long as the horse dream, but had given up on many, many years ago. With the horses, and all they stood for, being taken away, God was about to give me something to replace that gaping hole in my life. He had already given them to me without me totally realizing where it would lead and the impact it would have on others.

Practically no one knew of the love I had for dogs, except my family. But even they didn't know how intense my desire was to show and breed the dogs. Most of my horse friends were surprised to discover that I had shown dogs back in the late 60's and early 70's; it was not a new venture for me. I'd just not had the time or opportunity to do so prior to this and Bill was always against it. Now that the work with the horses was taken away from me, I turned to my dogs. With Bill's illness, and the dogs being right at and in the house, I was able to still enjoy my animals while caring for him.

Beagles would never have been my choice for raising and showing, but since Bill had gotten Bonnie, it just followed that I got that show beagle puppy. God blessed my time with the beagles, giving me my first championship title with Talia. I cannot describe the excitement that gave me. As the years rolled on from there, I made other champions with her offspring. It was a sport and a time I thoroughly enjoyed. God gave me something wonderful and better for this point in my life. As I face some uncertainties in life at this writing, I am choosing to believe this assurance and look forward to even better things in the future.

Through a set of circumstances I won't take time to write about here, I gave one-half ownership and full custody of my champion male beagle, Trystan, to someone I didn't even know all that well. To think of giving up one of my dogs, was, unthinkable. And, yet, I knew in my heart my heavenly Father was prompting me to do just that. I sat in my chair, dumfounded and in disbelief of what was happening as I watched Jordan drive out of my driveway with that dog in his car. It seemed so wrong but I knew it was so right.

From that act of obedience to my Lord, a relationship grew that continues to bless both of us. Jordan has become like a grandson to me – one my entire family adores. He has encouraged me to move on with my beagles; He filled the need to have someone to talk to about the dogs and showing; someone with as much excitement about it as I have. He is now my partner in the beagle business and gives me assurance that my dogs will be properly taken care of should something happen to me.

While all of that was, and is, wonderful; the most amazing thing about the relationship is that I have had the opportunity to mentor Jordan in his spiritual walk. I have the pleasure of watching him continually grow in his love for God and in desire to become the man God desires for him to be. What a blessing God has given me with this young man.

As Jordan and I talk about all the wonderful things God has done for us with the dogs, our horse businesses, and our friendship, we have talked about the realization of a very important lesson. The dogs and horses (Jordan makes his living training dressage horses) and the relationships we've formed through them, are not the means to the end. They are tools God uses to give opportunity to share Him with those we meet and spend time with. He uses our relationships through these animals to spread His gospel. The animals are blessings from Him, but they are His to use for His purposes and I am thrilled each time I see Him do that!

Chapter Forty

YEA, THOUGH I WALK...YET AGAIN

(Another deep, dark, valley to traverse)

1 Corinthians 7:39: "A woman is bound to her husband as long as he is alive." (NIV)

When I was 17 years old, I stood before family and friends and made a vow before God to stay with my husband ..."in sickness and in health - 'till death do us part". I had no clue in what way I would be tested to keep that vow; if I were to ever be tested at all. It meant little to me at the time.

There were many times throughout our marriage when I contemplated divorce or at least separation. Sometimes the constant bickering and fighting were just too much to take. To be honest, I didn't think a lot about that vow during those occasions: I would think about it on a regular basis years later as I had reason to honor my commitment.

Bill's illness progressed as is the nature of the disease. It moved from his being close to "normal" to making bigger and bigger mistakes as the months and years rolled by. He still wanted to help on the ranch, even after I got him away from the business. He was adamant that he could still operate the tractors and heavy equipment. He very much wanted to cut hay as he had for years. That would have been a disaster and likely have resulted in damage to the equipment and perhaps worse. For close to two years I would have to oversee everything he did and try to distract him from doing things that usually ended up badly. He was a very determined man and it was not easy to keep him in check. It was a blessing when he forgot enough about doing certain things that he lost interest in them. I was losing any sort of life of my own as he demanded more and more of my time and attention.

A sad day came when he sat in the loader and couldn't remember how to start it. On one occasion he tried to put gas into a diesel tractor; he would head to the wrong field with the wrong piece of equipment to do who knows what. It's a good thing I had a four-wheeler by that time as I never could have kept up with him without it.

It was becoming harder and harder for him to find his way around when driving and his driving was getting a bit scary. Eventually when he failed a psychological test at the doctor's office he had to take a driving test, which he failed, and thus lost his license. Very often he asked me when he could take the test again and get his license back. He was sure he could pass it: He couldn't understand how he had failed it. It broke my heart. His inability to drive added a huge burden to my already overloaded schedule as now he wasn't able to run any errands for me – I would have to do it all.

Knowing the day would come eventually when I would have to find some place he could go to get the care he needed, I researched methods of payment for a period of two years or more. I ran down every lead every person suggested to me; none would work. Everyone was sure their idea would pan out for me and I became weary. It just wasn't going to happen and I knew it. I had no idea how I would ever do it, but I had a sense of peace knowing God would take care of it when I needed it. We made little enough to get assistance, but as I did have income from the arena, we didn't qualify. It made no difference that since I could no longer generate income from training, the ranch was barely paying its own bills. I had to declare gross income. The bottom line is I was unable to get any help without paying for it. Due to the financial losses and the position we were in, that, too, was impossible. The only hope would be to find an organization that would care for him and wait for the money. That would be realized by signing our home and other assets over as collateral, letting the state take care of him, and then take those assets when he died. I would lose it all, especially if he was in a nursing home for any length of time. I talked to many people who had relatives in a nursing home and it cost them well over $200,000 for just a couple of years. I thanked God just about on a daily basis for one more day that I was able to care for him at home and didn't have to worry about signing my life away.

Unable to pursue help for him in that manner, I plugged away taking care of him, day by day and asking for God's leading and strength; and waiting. Bill was my constant companion: Everywhere I went; he went. Every day I was amazed that I was still able to do it. His symptoms became more varied and more serious. There was a time when, for close to a year, he was able to get on a little bus and go to the Senior Center in Union City for a few hours four days a week. He loved it; he got a good, hot meal there, interacted with people, and I got a few hours to do all the work that needed done here. He began wanting to be with me more and more and would call me up to come and get him. I was still able to talk him into waiting out the day until the bus brought him home. When he started leaving the home to try to come home, or beg someone to bring him home, they said he couldn't come back anymore. Now I had no reprieve and I felt trapped. I felt my life too was ebbing away. I felt I would never be free again.

His beloved Beagle, Bonnie, was still Bill's constant companion and for the better part of his disease he was still able to take her for walks down to the woods and back. I always timed those walks so that I would know if I should go looking for him, but I never had to. He did come back without her once though and when I inquired about it he told me he had turned her loose in the woods. I was not happy with that but she did come home in a timely fashion. Bonnie slept with Bill and was still quite a comfort for him.

In June of 2015 Bonnie was diagnosed with tumors on her lungs that were making it difficult for her to breathe and causing her to cough a lot. I could not bear the thought of taking her away from Bill and questioned God's timing in the matter. "Didn't he need her more now than ever? Couldn't you wait another year?" I asked God. Bonnie couldn't wait. Bill & I went to visit Jordan for a few days and while we were gone, Bev took care of having her put to sleep and buried at the edge of the back yard. She did a great job of it and the gravesite is quite pretty with a big unique-shaped rock over it as a marker. We plant flowers around it and beautify it even more. I could not bring myself to tell Bill that Bonnie was gone, and I didn't know how I would handle that. The first time he said he wanted to take her for a walk, I said to him, "You know, she always gets to go with you. Why don't you give another one a walk?" He would agree and I would put Bonnie's harness on Talia and let him take her. He was quite content to do so.

While I continued to question God's timing in losing Bonnie, I was to find out it was rather perfect after all. Bill never missed her and it was to the point that she would not have been able to stay with him in his room any longer for various reasons. A few months after she was gone, I showed him her gravesite and asked him about her. He couldn't remember her.

When Bill couldn't drive anymore I got him a bicycle so that he could at least get out and do something. He developed a real liking to riding it and for a time it was fun for him and a break for me when he would head down the road to be gone a half hour or so. He always went straight down the road and straight home. For several months I didn't have to worry about him on those excursions, but that all stopped when he began to get lost. The first time he got lost, he was found over nine miles from home – at dusk! If not for God having someone recognize him, and Bill still being able to tell him his name, I don't know how that would have ended. Many of us were searching a four mile radius around the ranch to no avail. In time I had to take steps to keep him off his bike. That got to be so difficult that the last time he literally ran away from me on it, I left it at the neighbor's so he couldn't do that anymore.

It was becoming more and more difficult to care for him as he required more and more care. He now was at about 195 pounds; me 5'2" and 125. He was becoming unsteady on his feet and I was his support. He required more and more supervision and if I was out of his sight, he would sneak out the door and take off on his bike or walk if it wasn't here, but he was going somewhere. I had to hide my vehicle as it was the same color as his had been and he insisted it was his. No amount of explanation would convince him otherwise.

Into about year nine of the disease things had progressed to the point where Bill needed constant supervision. Within the next year, I was unable to leave him alone in one room and go to another without him trying to make his escape. Nights were getting more difficult as he would be confused about what time of the day it was and try to leave the house. I set up door alarms so I would know if he was leaving his room. I feared getting so tired I would sleep through them and he would get out. I was almost panicky about it in the cold of winter. If he got out without me knowing it, he could get lost in the yard and freeze to death. I did not sleep much for close to a year.

He began hallucinating – seeing his parents in the house and then wondering where they went – actually looking for them. He would try very hard to convince me someone was waiting in the driveway for him and he needed to get out there and go with them. He would get quite upset when I wouldn't agree with him.

The next year was one in which I felt imprisoned. I do not like to be indoors as a rule, but almost cannot bear to be inside when the weather is good. I had ranch things to do and now couldn't get outside to do any of them. I couldn't even take a walk with my dogs. I was drowning in the enormity of the situation I found myself in. I was trapped in whatever room he needed to be in at the time, eyes always attentive to his moves. Even a bathroom break for me was becoming hard to take as he would see it as an opportunity to make a break for it. Pretty much alone, the task was becoming overwhelming. Everything I needed to do in the house pretty much had to wait until he went to bed, costing me more sleep.

A bright spot in my life during the last years with Bill was my sister, Bev, moving in with me. She had been unable to reconcile differences with her husband and proceeded with a divorce. Having a number of horses and a dog to take with her, my home was the logical place for her to move to. I had a barn for her horses, a place for her dog and the basement - that had been finished for some time and previously used to house the office's - became her home. She had privacy and all she needed. She took over doing my horse chores which enabled me to better care for Bill and gave me a tremendous peace of mind. When he reached the point of needing more care to diaper before bed and on occasion when I couldn't get him into the shower, she would help me. I didn't need her often, but I couldn't have done it without her when I did need her. She would often get supplies for me while she was on an outing, saving me the trouble of trying to get Bill and myself out to get them.

During his last year he forgot his children and eventually, on one occasion, even forgot me. In the fall of 2015, I questioned if he would make Christmas, but he seemed to rally for a period. I could take him to Laura Lee's on occasion to get a reprieve but that usually didn't work too well as he would get restless and just get up to go home. He was hard to stop. I would have to go get him. On one such visit, he had a really good day and was able to help them stack firewood. He felt so good and was so pleased to be of help. Around the same time, while he was taking one of the dogs for a walk to our woods, he came across Randy and Brenda cutting up firewood. He stopped to help and even told Brenda to take a break as he would do it for her. There were wonderful times for his kids and the last they would have with him in that manner.

He made it through Christmas better than I thought he would and I rejoiced that he was able to do so. After the holidays, he seemed to spiral downward. It got so that I had to feed him often as he couldn't remember how to do it himself; he had to start wearing diapers at night (and eventually during the day). No matter how much padding or how thick the diapers were he would wake up in the morning urine-soaked from his head to his lower buttocks – sometimes beyond. My first task each morning as he awoke was to get him undressed and into the shower, then tackle the arduous task of getting him re-dressed, put his bedding in the washer and move on to getting his breakfast. Only by the grace of God was I able to do all this.

By middle February it was getting more and more difficult to care for him. I had to have Bev help me a few times a week to get his diapers on at night and even had to have Brenda come one morning and help me get him into the shower. She shouldn't have had to see her father-in-law that way. Bill fell in the bathroom twice and I was unable to get him up by myself as now he didn't know how to be of any help himself. He would just lie there and be almost 200 pounds of dead weight. I called for my son to come help: He was shocked at what he saw.

I needed to make a trip to NC and it was impossible for me to take Bill anymore. I made arrangements for him to stay in a personal care home about 11 miles down the road from our home. While I was only going to be gone for a few days, I paid for six weeks to assure he would have a room in case he needed it longer, (he had gotten the last available one and I wanted to make sure it wasn't promised to someone else and then find out I needed it for him) but I secretly felt I would bring him home when I got back. The morning of the day I was to take him, was the hardest yet by far as I tried to get him from his bed to the shower and dressed. Uncannily I felt this would be the last time as I was no longer physically able to do it. I didn't know how I would take care of him after that, but I knew I couldn't continue as I was. It was the last time I showered and dressed him. Later that day I had to take him for some bloodwork before dropping him off at the home and almost couldn't do it. He was in a wheelchair by that time and unable to help himself in and out of it. I only have an Excursion to drive and getting in and out of that was extremely difficult. I felt so alone.

It ended up that he never left the personal care home. In the few days I had left him there, he sank even lower into the grip of the disease. Hospice made trips to the home for other patients and saw Bill among them. They called me requesting a meeting: We had a meeting in which they told me they wanted to take Bill as one of their patients. After hearing what they had to offer, I agreed. I felt a sense of relief having even more people now looking out for his welfare. Each week he got noticeably worse.

One time when I was visiting him and he was sitting in a recliner, I laid my head on his chest and after moving back from that position asked him if he knew who I was. He looked at me lovingly but with some confusion in his eyes – and finally said, "I don't know who you are but I know you are someone I love." He couldn't come up with my name but he knew that. It broke my heart.

I was able to visit him pretty much every day and was astonished at how rapidly he was declining. I wondered how long he would still be with us. The day before Easter was a summer-like Saturday and I was doing a barrel racing clinic at the ranch that ran well into the afternoon. I was tired but did a few things around the house and then asked Bev if she wanted to go for ice cream as I was going to run to Waterford to deposit the funds from the clinic. She did. My plan was to go visit Bill in the morning while everyone else was in church.

Randy had gone to see his dad on Friday evening and got to spend some quality time with him alone. Laura Lee went early Saturday afternoon and likewise had that 'alone' time with him. That gave me a sense of comfort inasmuch as I wouldn't see him that day. On my way back from Waterford, Laura Lee called me and told me her dad wasn't doing well and I should probably see him now. Agreeing, I dropped Bev off at the road in front of the house and continued on down to the home, arriving just after 7:00 in the evening.

Bill didn't look good as he lay in bed pretty much unaware of what was going on around him and he wasn't breathing normally. He looked at me but was unable to communicate. I cranked the head of his bed up a bit and called the hospice nurse. She said she would be there as soon as she could. I mentioned his breathing and she responded with, "that's the death rattle." I don't know how I felt as those words swam around in my brain. I spent the next hours singing to him and praying with him; I sat there and watched him die. It wasn't right, I thought. He died shortly before the calendar and clock would have declared Easter Sunday.

Due to someone's mistake that obviously resulted as a miscommunication between the hospital and our family doctor, our privacy was breeched and the hospital turned over all of Bill's medical records to our life insurance company even though they didn't even ask for them. When they discovered he had Lyme Disease, had had cancer. And now had Alzheimer's, they dropped his insurance. I had absolutely no money with which to bury him or to take care of my needs. Through the generosity of friends, I was able to have him cremated and give him a very nice funeral.

I sang "Serenaded By Angels" for him at the funeral. It was a song that was so appropriate for the occasion.

Bill had a favorite locust sprout in the front of the house – way too close to the house to grow there. I told him I had to remove it and it upset him a great deal so I let it go, knowing it was only a matter of time before I could do what needed to be done. In the spring of his death, I replanted that hardy stick of a tree over some of Bill's ashes right behind the rock at Bonnie's grave. It is flourishing and growing well. I look at it as part of Bill still being here. It is fitting his and Bonnie's remains are together, but bittersweet as I stop by each time I'm mowing the lawn, shed some tears, and move on, "'til death do us part."

Chapter Forty-One

THE STRAW THAT BROKE THE CAMEL'S BACK – ALMOST

Psalm 119:147: "I rise before the dawning of the morning, and cry for help; I hope in Your word." (NKJV)

With Bill's many sicknesses and depression, things began falling apart in the business. He was making huge mistakes in job related issues and it was costing us dearly in every aspect of the business. There were some serious business and financial issues that were like a weight tied around my neck. I spent what money Bill & I had for our retirement on paying business debts, including saving equipment from being repossessed, (two pieces were at one point and we had to bail them out) keeping up insurance and paying taxes. I feared bankruptcy and I *knew* it was inevitable. I was sure we were going to lose everything but more so I did not want to go through the process and face my creditors. I needed answers from God but mostly I needed that peace I had long sought. In the midst of all of these issues I was dealing with Bill's progressing disease – one that became more demanding by the day.

I blamed most of my problems on the business with its demands and problems. "If only I didn't have to have anything to do with it, life would be so much better" I would tell myself. I would have little to fear and be anxious about I reasoned. Thinking through it again as I write, I believe I finally understand the matter of the business. My problem was not the business per se, even though it was problem riddled and a pressure cooker of stress, but rather that the business revealed *my* problem; that being one of basic sin in my life - sin expressed in fear, guilt, and lack of trust in my heavenly Father. I believe it revealed the true hindrance of the joy-filled life He wants for me – the reason I found no real peace though heaven knows how hard I tried.

In 2008, everything we had on the ranch was debt-free. I took major pride in that and it was my biggest sense of security. We had accomplished this feat through funds from gas well royalties – from the four wells on the property, selling horses, training horses, events held at the ranch, and even cashing in an insurance policy. During these difficult times, we, personally, were without debt. I felt a great sense of much-needed security because of it.

Due to the company being a family business, all business deals were required to include personal guarantees. This included every loan we incurred, whether for a bank business mortgage or an equipment company from whom we made purchases. While I hadn't given this much thought as I tried to keep business somewhat separated from home, it meant we actually had no security at all. Should the business fail, they could sell our home *first* to recoup their losses. Therefore, while we were "proud" that we had this lovely place mortgage free, in essence we had no security from the bank and their legal claims to our personal property. This caused even greater fear, leading to more physical problems for me.

The fear this put in my heart was indescribable; the stark terror that I lived with on a daily basis, unimaginable. Understanding that if we failed to make bank payments and they decided to move on us, they could sell our home to recoup their loss was far more than I could bear emotionally. Where would I go? What would happen to my horses and my dogs? I took on the responsibility of my employee's futures and I made decisions to protect them. I couldn't bear to tell them they were going to lose their jobs and their health insurance. How could I live through that? If I had let them go and given them to God then I may not have struggled so much and so long with them. The fear of what people would think, what my family would assume when "I" failed, what our competitors would say was crippling. Would it all come back on "She did this or she didn't do that?" I was convinced it was all going to be placed on my shoulders.

December of 2009 found me at my wit's end. I was so emotionally charged over all that had been and was still going on in the business that I was crumbling under the weight of it all, often complaining to the Lord that I could take no more. I knew God would take care of me: I had watched Him do it over and over, but I was unable to give my fears to Him and unable to trust Him. This was so big! Peace still eluded me. Everything was now on my shoulders. Bill was no longer able to be of any help in the business and had to be kept from it. I was busy taking care of him and trying to save what I could of the business to leave something for our son who often blamed all its woes on me. I had the ranch to run with its responsibilities. I felt I was in a pit; and had no way out. I was thinking seriously of signing myself into the hospital mental health ward, hoping for some rest and a way to escape my problems. If I had thought it through I would have realized it wouldn't have helped other than I might have been put on some medication that could have made me feel better, but without solving my problems. That wouldn't really have been helpful. I didn't know what to do. I just knew I couldn't go on the way I was.

While I was working hard at trusting God more and more, I was still desperately seeking His peace, the peace the Bible and godly men and women talked about. It still eluded me. I only had momentary periods of peace which were as a direct result of some relief in a difficult area. Since the difficulties never end, the peace was infrequent and short-lived and resulted in a virtual roller coaster ride of emotions as a result. I still didn't sleep well – awaking often completely tormented by anxiety over the business; its failures and needs.

I felt like 'one more straw' would break my back. I thought this was all I could expect from life – a constant struggle to follow God and to work at trusting Him to take care of me: A period of life wherein I would beg for help from Him; He would eventually (in my time table) come through for me and I would immediately beg for relief from the next problem. It was an ongoing circle of life for me. I'd been praying and praying. I was getting no closer to the peace I needed even though I thought I was doing everything right. I didn't know what else to do. I was sinking deeper and deeper into depression. I would say "again" but I don't think I ever fully recovered from the previous depression. I had been plagued with it all my life.

During this critical struggle Bev gave me a gift that God knew I needed. It was a small book; a devotional. Its title is "*Jesus Calling*" by Sarah Young. I've read countless books throughout my lifetime and have gleaned much from many, but this little book was about to change my life. It wasn't just the content, although it is very good – but it was the manner in which it was written; written in a personal way; written for each day as if recording two people who were having a conversation. It inspired me to begin journaling each day.

Up until that time, I hit the ground running each and every day of my life. I am a morning person and I work hard and heavy first thing off. I felt I never had time to sit down and read my Bible in the morning, although when weather was not conducive to being outside, I would spend that time with it had read through the Bible about six times by this period and credited it for literally saving my life. My Bibles are marked with notes, dates, and highlighting; the promises He gives being my saving grace, but now God was asking me to do something more. I just didn't have time. There were too many things to do and deal with on a daily basis and I needed to be busy with them. I would read it later in the day when I had more time. Now, God was telling me to take the first part of my day and spend it with Him and His Son. I wasn't sure I would be able to do that. I had too much to do, (some things (like weed spraying) before the wind kicked up which it does daily here and very early) but, out of desperation, I began. I had to try something.

The journaling came so easy it surprised me and I found benefit in it from the first day. My way of spending this time is to record my thoughts and even my actions over the past 24 hours, thanking Him for His blessings and petitioning Him for my needs. When I am finished with that, I read a devotional that never fails to completely, accurately, and specifically address my needs: I record that below my writings. It is a two-way conversation and I find it therapeutic. Recording the blessings reminds me of His care for me; reading His response to my needs encourages me and gives me hope. Almost from the first day, I eagerly spend my first time in the morning with my Lord. I looked forward to it then and I still do. It became so important to me that a few weeks after starting, and in the hospital, I was desperate to continue. My right arm was in a sling from the shoulder surgery and the other swollen into a bent position caused by the technician infiltrating my left arm with dye as he missed the vein while giving me a cat scan to locate the blood clots in my lungs. In spite of it all I still found a way to type on my computer and do my journaling with God. I did not want to miss a day. In the past seven years I don't believe I've missed a dozen days. It is that important to me and I know it is to the King as well.

As I spent that time with my Lord each morning, my entire perspective on life and my circumstances began to change. I'd like to say my circumstances changed for the better, but they didn't (just my perspective on them). In most areas of my life they remained the same and some got continually worse. But *I* began to change.

This practice began to encourage me and give me hope: It helped me realize that God has a plan for my life and will still take care of me. I stopped worrying about what I wasn't getting done while spending the time with Him and discovered once again that God is the redeemer of time and He will never owe me anything. What I had thought would put a big wrinkle in my day's productivity, did no such thing. I realized quickly that I didn't lose a thing but actually gained as I seemed to get just as much done in a day as ever – often more. Starting each day in communion with the Savior gave me the strength I needed to face the day.

God was and is so patient with me! He took care of me over and over, even when I didn't trust Him any more for the current issue than I had the one before. He never gave up on me and constantly proved His love for me. With His help and our new-found relationship, I slowly learned to give things up to Him and to build a trust in Him; trusting Him for the outcome. Then, and now, I need to be reminded that He loves me, and while I may not understand the whys of what is happening in my life, I can know that whatever comes out of my circumstances will be for my betterment and for God's glory. When I can focus on that truth, I can trust Him. It has been a long, hard road to travel to this point and I'm not at the end yet. As I am writing this, I have no idea if I will be able to remain in the home Bill and I built or if I will be forced to sell it and move elsewhere.

There are many hazards yet in my path, but I'm learning that in all things, He can be trusted. I have experienced the peace of God. I've learned how to experience His peace when the world is shouting doom and destruction. I have found true peace. I found it in the eye of the storm, not the calm that follows the storm. It is a peace the world cannot understand – a peace that is only found in God. It is in surrender of the things that belong to Him in the first place, not trying with all my might to hang onto them. I found it is only attainable by giving all to Him: Everything. It comes with trusting Him to make the right decisions for all concerned. It isn't my place to provide for my son or my friends or employees. Each situation needed to be handed over to him. I needed to learn to trust Him with them as well. Slowly, I learned that truth and began applying it to my life. Only with His help, His grace; His mercy, have I been able to not only survive but to live. I have learned to find blessings in each day no matter what else may cross my path: I have learned to enjoy each day instead of surviving each day. Oh, incredible, blessed peace!

Chapter Forty-Two

YOU BE THE ONE

1 Corinthians 15:10: "But by the grace of God, I am what I am, and His grace toward me was not in vain." (NKJV)

Many years ago as I was just beginning to go through the countless trials that lay ahead, I was arguing with the Lord about them on a regular basis. I often asked Him why I had to go through so many. Apart from the obvious answer – that I had asked for and needed patience - (Romans 5:3b "and we know that tribulation produces patience…"), He pointed me to 2 Corinthians 1: 3, 4, wherein it states "God…and the One who so wonderfully comforts and strengthens us in our hardships and trials. And why does He do this? So that when others are troubled, needing our sympathy and encouragement, we can pass on to them this same help and comfort God has given us." (TLB)

I was not happy with Him pointing that out to me; I responded with "Let someone else be the one to help them. I do not want to go through all this frustration and heartache just to do that. It doesn't seem fair to me." He could have quit on me right there, but thankfully He did not. He did not because He knew, while I did not, that fulfillment would come to me when I was doing that very thing. I certainly was not happy with many of the ways He chose to get me to that point, however. One of the ways He made it clear to me what would really give me that sense of fulfillment was speaking at Christian Women's Clubs. Sharing His faithfulness to me with others and encouraging them to trust Him as I have learned to is a privilege beyond description.

I have been blessed to have opportunity to encourage others on a one-on-one basis as well. I discovered that I am not alone in my struggles in so many areas. While I have had many experiences I could share God's provision through, I've discovered one of the primary needs from other women is learning how to deal with situations concerning husband and home without losing their Christian witness. Many are dealing with issues where needed help and support are not offered or given from whom they need it. They want to know how to get this help without nagging or fighting. Some need to know simply how to live a Christian lifestyle in severely difficult circumstances. I certainly do not have all the answers, but I'm happy to share with them what God has shown me.

God taught me much in my personal life I could then share with others. As mentioned elsewhere, Bill felt nothing on the ranch was his responsibility, yet I would find myself in need of his help from time to time. I learned to be very careful in how I asked for that help (boy did that go against the grain!) and even more careful in my reaction to his response, whatever it might be. Most times any request I made was not favored with a reaction of any kind for several days. By a large margin when it did come, that response was generally negative: "no time; not a good time; can't do it"; and a number of other similar answers were generally what I was given.

If I had any comment or argument, that would ensure he would not consider doing it but would use it as his excuse not to. As I was in the habit of trying to get my point across, it was quite difficult to just accept his answer then go to God and talk to Him about it. As I did, though, God would convey to me that He would take care of the matter if I left it to Him and did not compromise my declaration of following Him.

At this time God also gave me a new concept to swallow and follow. He told me He wanted to love my husband *through* me! Whoa! Use me to channel love to a husband who was not meeting my needs and was downright difficult most of the time? While I did not want any part of that task, knowing in my heart just how unfair that was to ask of me, I knew that if God told me something, it was because it was the way it would work and that ultimately it would be good for me as well. I reluctantly agreed to be willing to be made willing and in time I began to practice what I preached, so to speak.

Once again, God was right. I watched Bill make subtle chances in his dealings with me – oh so few and so far between at first, but changes, nonetheless. I watched with amazement in that as I did as God commanded me, He channeled my husband's interest to do the very things necessary to take care of my needs. I marveled as this state of affairs developed over time to the point that at times I went to God first without even telling my husband of my needs, yet God motivated him to take care of situations without my even asking. What a difference this can make in a relationship! I eventually learned to tell God of my needs before I told my husband. I knew He would work it out best.

One important key is realizing that, should my husband fail to meet my needs, I need not despair. God will supply them by other means. I have no need to worry, fret, or fuss. He will honor the sincere seeker of His wonderful provision!

Knowing that God ultimately has the say in any situation and being willing to accept His decisions took a lot of pressure off our marriage. When I was disappointed because things were not being done the way I wanted or in the time I had planned, I learned to talk to my Lord about it and to realize He will take care of it in His way and His timing, which are always best. Handling situations this way eliminated the anger and frustration previously bestowed upon my husband.

My gaining understanding that my heavenly Father will see to my needs, whether through my husband or by other means relieved my husband of the pressure of living up to my demands. He could then concentrate more on hearing God, rather than me, and God has a much better way of molding one into the man he ought to be.

While I still have a problem with unfairness, I now trust the Lord more in those situations knowing that if I give them to Him, all will be well. I am still in awe of the changes He made in my husband, as I put my desires aside and simply tried to become what God wanted me to be.

This revelation totally transformed our marriage. After 35 years of marriage, we were able to work together without arguing, actually even enjoying it. Bickering and arguing became things of the past. Anger became a very rare and quickly dispelled emotion. Our last 20 years of marriage were spent caring for and about one another as we should have all along. The wonderful experience of a good marriage wiped out all the previous damaging years we spent fighting one another. I was amazed to realize just how much my husband loved and adored me, once he felt safe to let me know.

My husband believed me to be the greatest human being on earth and was not afraid to tell me and others of that belief. He cherished me: he loved nothing better than to find ways to take care of me. I am in awe of the very situation I found myself in, as I never believed for a moment this could happen.

In Joel 2:25 God says, "I will repay you for the years the locusts have eaten…and you will praise the name of the Lord your God…" He restored many years for Bill and me and we were quick to praise His name! A life turned over to God can change!

But even more than the changes in my husband, I am astonished at the changes God has made in me. As I think of the things that used to bother me and cause problems in our relationship and beyond and as I enjoy the peace that only comes from surrendering to God, I am amazed at those changes. I regret the years I spent impatient with my children over things now so trivial that were so important to me at the time. I have experienced much emotional healing over the issues that used to dominate my thinking as I accept the peace He has to offer.

I am no longer insecure, but very secure in the knowledge that He loves me and wants what is best for me. I am secure as He has taught me not to strive to be perfect but to strive to know Him. I've gained security as I see the changes he's made not only in my personality but in my heart. I do not have to act a certain way as He has changed me to *be* a certain way. In humility, as it was not my nature, I am pleased to say that what I felt was impossible, God has accomplished. God has developed that meek and gentle spirit in me. My husband would be the first to tell you that. At one point he remarked to me, "Joan, you are too patient!" I know firsthand what God can do with a life surrendered to Him. To God be the glory!

I have many experiences to share with others of God's provision, love, care, and concern for me. I have been a speaker for Christian Women's Club meetings for many years now. While I had to put that avenue of sharing on hold for the time spent caring for Bill, I have begun to minister in that way again. It is one of the things I enjoy the most. Thank You, Lord, for not giving up on me when I so selfishly wanted to be left alone.

Oh, the unfathomable grace God has bestowed on me. No one knows better than me what He has kept me from; all the possibilities for destroying my testimony for Him, for living an ineffective, wasted life, or worse yet, ending that life prematurely. That is what the enemy wanted, but praise God; He had other plans for me and held onto me until I was ready to fulfill them for Him.

These are just some of the things I am privileged to share with others who are struggling with the same circumstances.

God told me all those years ago He would someday want me to share His matchless grace with those who came into my life and needed help and comfort. How thankful I am He did not give up on me when I balked at the idea. What a privilege it has become to do just that very thing. My life has never been more fulfilled. All I can say is, "Oh, Lord, use me!"

Chapter Forty-Three

THE RANCH (AND ME) IN GOD'S HANDS

Proverbs 2:8: "For He guards the course of the just and protects the way of His faithful ones." (NIV)

As mentioned previously in this book, I struggled with the horses' place in my life. Did they have one? What and where was it? Was I ever going to get the chance to use them for Him? Some days I felt they had no real purpose. I wanted to believe God gave them to me just for my pleasure yet I couldn't quite accept that. I still longed to use them for Him but finally was willing to wait for His direction and timing.

Over the years things changed dramatically. For so many years we felt we would never have many Christian friends who were also horse lovers. We now have an abundance of them, with God adding to them regularly. Camp Halo used Everwind Ranch and its facilities for ten years, ministering to thousands of children during that period. "Horse people" have started to ask me to pray for them. I have had Christian messages given at clinics held here and I have given such messages at clinics held by others here at our facility. I have even had occasion to speak at events held in arenas away from home. My ranch website, www.everwind.com has a Christian page with words to encourage living a Christian lifestyle.

Recently a student's mother approached me and asked if they could start coming on Thursdays at 5:00 P.M. Assuming she was requesting that slot for a lesson, I interrupted her and told her I was sorry but that was Bible Study time. She responded with, "That's what we want to come for!"

Just this very day (as I pen these words) I had the opportunity to lead a teenage girl to the Lord! She has been coming to the ranch to have a place to be around horses and has attended the last two Bible studies. Because of her love for horses, and God's provision of them here, she found the Savior!

God has given me opportunity to make an impact on children and adults alike in the horse arenas and in the arena of life as I coach them. Counseling opportunities have developed with both students and friends through the association with the horses. We started a Cowboy Church that has had an impact and are looking for God's direction on moving forward with it.

Oh, He is using the horses alright. He had it planned all along. Like the speaking opportunities, He was just waiting until I allowed enough changes to be made in me to be useful in His plans.

When one thing is taken away, He gives another. When one dream is surrendered, He fulfills another to a greater extent than one could imagine.

And now, while not necessarily using *ranch* animals, He is using the gift of dogs. It gives me opportunity to cultivate more relationships that result in occasion to share My Lord with them.

I see a thread in my life – a golden one – that often weaved in and out, rarely on a straight line, but yet unbroken; it is always connected to the One who is my All in all. I now see more and more areas where it is not crooked, but straight from my heart to the Savior's. My goal is to have it a straight line and to preserve it.

"But by the grace of God, I am what I am, and His grace toward me was not in vain." Thank you, Jesus!

It's not about the dogs: It's not about the horses: It's not about me....It is about Him!

"It's not about you, Joan."

Chapter Forty-Four

AFTERGLOW

Psalm 4:8a: "I will both lay me down in peace and sleep." (NKJV)

Shortly before putting the final touches on this manuscript I sat in the living room, waiting for bedtime. The last project I undertook for the day was spent working another four hours on the enormous job of pressure-washing the original barn on this property. It is 102' long and 36' wide and I am preparing it for a new coat of paint. It is hard and tedious work as I am cleaning every square inch of the cement block walls, removing almost every spot of old paint from them. I have been working on it for a couple of weeks, have prepared the one long end, and now am trying to finish up for this first round by getting the high walls on the west end of it ready as well. I am expecting to have someone come spray paint it in about four days.

It is tiring work and with all the other work I do on a daily basis, this day it made me especially tired as the evening waned and gave way to nighttime. I cannot go to bed until the dogs are taken care of for the last time late enough that they will be comfortable for the night. It would do me no good to go to bed earlier anyway as I would just wake up that much sooner or not sleep well.

I sat on the couch busying myself with a Matlock program on TV and checking things out on my computer trying to stay awake until I could justify going to bed. The significant thing about this entire matter – and what prompted this extra writing – was that I *longed* for bed! I so looked forward to going to bed and having a peace-filled night of however much sleep I got. I couldn't wait to go to bed! It wasn't long ago that I dreaded bed, fearing the anxiety the night would bring as I worried about the next day, not wanting to face it as I wasn't able to deal with the problems I knew it held. Now, each and every night I look forward to the rest it gives me both physically and mentally and look with anticipation to what the next day will bring, knowing that You have gone ahead and prepared the best one for me.

In my entire life, I have never been in a more 'needy' position. I am alone with a magnitude of issues to deal with from now fixing things on the lawn mower and skidsteer that I never dreamed I would have to, or could do, and constantly working on ideas to keep up with things and make them profitable. I have no one to turn to for help for those things as I did in the past. I have nowhere near enough financial resources to get through one month at a time and yet.

You; You have proven You will take care of me. You give me a song in the night and peace-filled sleep. You have taken me from anxiety and fear-filled sleepless nights to longing to curl up against your bosom and sleep completely safe in Your arms. I can now sing, "Because He lives, I can face tomorrow…." and mean every word! Words cannot express the differences You have made in my life. You have shown me I do not need to give in to depression and self-pity; that I do not need external, man-made help or ideas of how to find peace and *get by*. You are in the business of showing me the true way to peace that is found only in You and trusting You for my every need. Oh the joy of it all!

I heard a sermon on the radio recently and the testimony of a man who did not know Christ personally as he gave voice to what the message meant to him. He couldn't remember the message – although it was a good message. (I heard it as well.) From the message he remembered one line; a line that changed his life; a line I bring to mind very often since hearing it. The phrase that got through his exterior and to his heart was this: "You can trust the Man who died for you." I am learning the truth of those words. You can trust Him – for everything, including your very life. I'm learning how.

EPILOGUE

Jeremiah 29: 11 (NIV) For I know the plans I have for you," declares the LORD, "plans to prosper you and not to harm you, plans to give you hope and a future."

As I prepare to write "The End" on this manuscript, it is with reservation and a measure of sadness, as I believe my Father is nowhere near finished with me. I believe He still has plans for me – plans that will let me bring honor and glory to Him, as I desire.

Through my journey of life, so much of it was spent worrying about me, Joan, and my needs. God has lovingly taught me that in all events and circumstances; all blessings He gave and continues to give are tools that I am, in turn, to use to further His purposes; not mine. Just as He already redeemed the time taken from me when caring for Bill, He is redeeming the time of my life wasted on my own desires. I pray He gives me the opportunity to make some of it up to Him.

I am less than a month from 75 years old as I write this. There is much that space did not allow me to record and my days continue to be full of wonderment as He continually takes care of me in ways I never dreamed. I hate to quit writing but I must put "The End" somewhere. I have dreams, still; dreams of just what He might want to do with and through me for the remainder of the time He has allotted me to spend here on *terra firma*. I don't know if my dreams are His dreams or if they will be fulfilled. I do know He has the best plan, and He will work it out for my good and His glory as I continue to yield my life to Him.

It never was about *me*.